THE
LOW-HIGH THEORY
OF INVESTMENT

How to Make Money in the Stock
Market—and Keep It

THE
LOW-HIGH THEORY
OF INVESTMENT

How to Make Money in the Stock Market—and Keep It

SAMUEL C. GREENFIELD

Coward-McCann, Inc.
New York

This book is dedicated to my wife, Miriam, and my daughters, Joan and Ruth.

Only people are precious: Money is round and rolls hither and yon.

ACKNOWLEDGMENTS

I wish to thank Mrs. Esther Marcus, B.A.; Nathan I. Hodas, B.S., L.L.B.; the staff of Henry Schulman & Co., C.P.A., and Louis Bachner, B.C.S., C.P.A.; Miss Kathryn Keegan; and Mrs. Frances Kohan. Special thanks are due to my daughter Mrs. Ruth G. Zinn for the research.

Contents

Introduction

Investing is an adventurous occupation:
The lure of gain invites
The fear of loss threatens
Few are truly satisfied.

It is said that investors move from brokerage house to brokerage house as patients move from psychoanalyst to psychoanalyst. They are never satisfied. An investor buys a security and sells it at a handsome profit because he feels that it has reached the top of its market. Instead of dropping and leaving him with the satisfying vanity of his acute judgment, it continues to rise. This is enough to create the ulcer of regret and unhappiness. Or, he buys when he thinks the stock has reached its rock bottom price. It usually goes lower. Or, he may buy at the bottom and sell at the top. He makes a lot of money. The thought of paying so much in income taxes leaves him depressed. These built in frustrations, superimposed on the thrill to "beat the market," makes the game both exciting as well as hazardous.

There are many individuals who do well with their investments. They buy carefully, after adequate research, wait patiently, and sell when their profit objective has been reached. But, there are many others who do poorly. In 1963, for example, (this is the latest year for which statistics are available) there were almost 1 million 600 thousand people who ended the year with a net capital loss of almost *four billion dollars.*

This means that their losses exceeded their gains by four billion dollars. Lest one think that 1963 was an unusual year, here are the figures for the previous five years.

Net Losses from the Sale of Capital Assets

Year	Number of Returns	Net Capital Loss
1959	900,118	$1.9 billion
1960	1,154,339	2.4 billion
1961	1,097,455	2.3 billion
1962	1,599,445	3.8 billion
1963	1,595,319	4.0 billion

The cold statistics leave little impact, but the tragedies are implicit in each individual instance. How many homes were broken up? How many businesses were ruined? How many elderly, retired people suffered losses they could not afford?

There are many reasons why so many people lose so much. They want too much profit, too quickly, and too effortless. This explains why books that pretend to show people how to make a million, or two, or a hundred, are eagerly bought and avidly read. Everyone is looking for the easy path to riches.

This book does not intend to excite people to gamble by presenting old, shopworn ideas, in new garb. The objective is to shift the million six hundred thousand losers to the winning side, and to furnish them and those who do well with the tools to improve their judgment.

The investment approach in this book is based on logic and reasoning. Securities have been bought and sold for a long time. Certain patterns have been established. They can be studied and understood, the same as is done in physics and mathematics.

There are two aspects of this book that need explanation. First is the order of the chapters. They have been arranged in the order of importance to the practical investor. He wants a guide that will enable him to make profits, each and every year, safely and soundly. He wants to avoid costly errors.

The most important concept for successful investment is the "Spread-Theory," which appears in Chapter 1. This theory describes and analyzes the movement of securities and draws necessary conclusions. It predicts their probable annual range, within reasonable limits. It erects boundary lines within which investments can be made safely and profitably.

Second, how should the book be read? The first reading should be quick, without too much attention to tables, percentages or details. The objective is to become familiar with the approach. The second reading should be slower, with attention to details. Finally, the reader should take pencil and paper in hand and study the material. A good businessman does not rush into a contract on the basis of a hasty appraisal. He does a considerable amount of calculation before committing one penny. Investing funds should be approached with the same detailed care.

Division is used extensively. Using the slide rule makes the process simple. Buy an inexpensive one and read the instructions on division. It is quite easy.

Investing is full of excitement, thrills and frustration. There are numerous snares, enticingly embellished, that trap the anxious and uninformed. These can be avoided by learning the rules of the game and knowing how to apply them. Study the rules. Respect them. And enjoy the rich rewards that will result.

THE
LOW-HIGH THEORY
OF INVESTMENT

How to Make Money in the Stock
Market–and Keep It

1
The Low-High Spread

The Fashion Followers

It is unlikely that the crafty Cassius could have foreseen 2,000 years ago that stock market traders of the twentieth century would be blaming their losses on bad luck. The prophet was Shakespeare. He understood the frailties of human nature.

Many traders have little success with their investments. For a number of illogical reasons, they invariably buy at the wrong time. If they sold when they bought they would make fortunes. The only time their securities rise is when they contemplate buying them. Then the stocks keep going up day after day while they watch in anguish. Finally, exhausted, they can hold out no longer and succumb. From then on the stocks start falling. What demon haunts them?

There are many reasons why some people lose consistently. One of the most important is that they are the victims of the villain "fashion." The same pressure that dictates the clothing they wear and the cigarettes they smoke, determines what securities they buy and when they buy them. Examine some portfolios and you can date the purchases. U.S. Steel was probably bought in 1959 and 1960, Motorola in 1966, and Monsanto Chemical in 1965. It was during these years that these enjoyed the height of their popularity. They were the topic of "smart" conversation, made the most active list, received the best press, were discussed by the finest services, and enjoyed the most bizarre rumors. They were the "in stocks." Naturally, they were bought. Then they went out of style and were replaced by new, more romantic issues. Round and round goes the market.

Buying a security should be more than calling your broker and placing an order. That is the last step in a long series of steps. For many individuals, it is the second step. The first is hearing about the stock from a friend, neighbor, or associate. The second is to rush to the phone before it is too late, and order the stock bought at the market. The last is to sell it before the year ends for a tax loss.

Low-High Spread

One of the first things to do before buying a security is to study its historic trading pattern. Is it a volatile issue whose swings are wide, or is its activity confined to a narrow range? Once that is determined, the next question is, what is the price of the security now? Is it near the high of the year or the low? Has it already increased 100% from its lowest price? My personal experience is that whenever a client calls excitedly about a security, it is at the high of the year. No one ever calls to inquire about a stock when it is at its low.

There is an easy way to study the historic trading pattern of a security. The Standard & Poor reports on listed securities indicate, among other bits of information, the highest and lowest prices at which they sold each year. The facts can be arranged in tabular form, called a Low-High Spread chart. To illustrate, examine two securities, Standard Oil of New Jersey, representing the group that normally moves within a narrow trading range, and Zenith Radio Company, representing stocks whose swings are much wider.

Chart 1 indicates the percentage increase from the low to high of the *same year.* For Standard Oil of New Jersey, for example, the stock increased from $50 to *$63* in 1956 or *26%*. In 1957 the increase was 43%, etc.

Chart 1
Low-High Spread Chart
from Low to High of Same Year
(Adjusted for splits and stock dividends)

	Standard Oil New Jersey			Zenith Radio		
	Lowest Price Per Share	Highest Price Per Share	Percent Spread L-H	Lowest Price Per Share	Highest Price Per Share	Percent Spread L-H
1956	$50	$63	26%	$ 3	$ 4	33%
1957	48	69	43	3	4	33
1958	48	60	25	4	12	200
1959	46	59	28	10	23	130
1960	38	51	34	15	22	46
1961	41	52	27	16	41	156
1962	45	60	33	21	38	81
1963	58	77	33	26	42	62
1964	75	93	23	31	44	42
1965	74	90	22	31	61	97
1966	66	84	27	46	89	93
1967	59	71	20	48	72	50

Studying the annual percentage increase gives the investor valuable information. Standard Oil of New Jersey, for example, moved in a narrow range. During the eleven years in this study, the increase never reached 50%. In only 4 years did it rise above 30%. Under the circumstances, where the stock was purchased after it increased by as little as 25% from its low, it did not rise too much after that. It had gone just about as far as it could that year. Thereafter it started its annual descent. Many who purchased thousands of shares at or near the top must have been quite frustrated as they saw their "blue chip" fall.

Zenith presents a totally different picture. Its moves are wide. In the same eleven years its low-high spread was less than 50% in only 4 years. In 3 years it exceeded 100%. Buying it when it had increased by 30% from its low represented little risk. But when the security was purchased after it had increased 75 to 80% the risk increased, and kept increasing as the percentage rose.

One should know whether he is buying a security whose low-high spread is narrow or wide; also how narrow and how wide. History never repeats in precisely the same way. However, the past can be a useful guide.

The investor should learn an important lesson from these two representative charts. Each security has its own individual low-high spread pattern, from which it may stray occasionally, but which characterizes it. If the security is purchased near the lower area of its annual range it will probably do well. However, if it is purchased nearer the higher area, it will probably do poorly. There are always exceptions, but don't hope for them.

In fact, it would be wise, when making the chart, to write the word DANGER in dark red, above the area where the risk increases beyond the normal.

In the case of Standard Oil of New Jersey, the risk area is reached after the security has increased 20% or more above the year's low. In the case of Zenith, it is above 40%.

The Perennial Pattern

There is an important *similarity* between the two groups that is as significant as their *difference*. Each has its winter when it falls to its lowest price of the year and its summer when it reaches its highest.

The low-high table reveals a second important piece of information. It indicates the extent to which a security falls each year after it has reached its pinnacle. For example, after Standard Oil of New Jersey reached $63 per share in 1956, it fell to $48 the next year. It then climbed again to $69 only to drop to $48 in 1958. Zenith Radio pursued a similar course of action. It also rose to a high each year only to fall significantly the next, etc.

Revise Chart 1 by placing a series of oblique lines from the

high of one year to the *low of the following year.*

The oblique lines in Chart 2 indicate the drop from the high of one year to the low of the following. It's up and down, up and down, each and every year. In some years the low came first followed by the high and in others the high preceded the low.

Chart 2
Low-High Spread Chart
from High of One Year
to Low of Following Year
(Adjusted for stock dividends and splits)

	Standard Oil New Jersey		Zenith Radio	
	Lowest Price Per Share	*Highest Price Per Share*	*Lowest Price Per Share*	*Highest Price Per Share*
1956	$50 DOWN	$63	$ 3 DOWN	$ 4
1957	48	69	3	4
1958	48	60	4	12
1959	46	59	10	23
1960	38	51	15	22
1961	41	52	16	41
1962	45	60	21	38
1963	58	77	26	42
1964	75	93	31	44
1965	74	90	31	61
1966	66	84	46	89
1967	59	71	48	72

It might be useful, at this point, to introduce still another chart on the same "Yo-Yo" pattern (see page 22). What is the percentage increase from the low of one year to the low of the following?

In 1957 Standard Oil of New Jersey dropped to a low of $48 per share or $2 less than the low of $50 established in 1956. This represented a drop of 4%. In 1958 it fell back to its low of 1957, etc.

Chart 3
**Low-Low Spread Chart from Low of
One Year to Low of the Following Year
(Adjusted for splits and stock dividends)**

	Standard Oil of New Jersey		Zenith Radio	
Year	Lowest Price of Year	Percent Increase or Decrease	Lowest Price of Year	Percent Increase or Decrease
1956	$50		$ 3	
		−4%		0%
1957	48		3	
		0		33
1958	48		4	
		−4		150
1959	46		10	
		−17		50
1960	38		15	
		8		7
1961	41		16	
		10		31
1962	45		21	
		29		24
1963	58		26	
		29		19
1964	75		31	
		−1		0
1965	74		31	
		−11		48
1966	66		46	
		−12		5
1967	59		48	

Combining these figures with those in Chart 1 presents an interesting conclusion. It doesn't matter how high a security rose in any one year, if it fell substantially the following year. In the case of Standard Oil of New Jersey, the spread was 26% from the *low of 1956* to the *high of the same year* (Chart 1). The very next year the stock dropped to $48, which was 4% below the low of 1956.

Zenith Radio presents a similar picture. Although the security rose by 33% from the low of 1956 to the high that year, it dropped back to its previous low in 1957. Moving down the years note 1961 when the rise that year from low to high was 156%. However, the very next year it fell back to $21 which was only 31% above the previous year's *low*.

Charts 1 and 3 can be seen best by placing the percentages alongside one another.

Comparison Chart 4A
Low of One Year to High of Same Year (Chart 1)
vs. Low of One Year to Low of Following Year (Chart 3)
Standard Oil of New Jersey

Year	Percent Increase Low to High Same Year	Percent Increase or Decrease of Low of First Year to Low of Following Year	
1956	26%	−4%	1956-7
1957	43	0	1957-8
1958	25	−4	1958-9
1959	28	−17	1959-60
1960	34	8	1960-1
1961	27	10	1961-2
1962	33	29*	1962-3
1963	33	29*	1963-4
1964	23	−1	1964-5
1965	22	−11	1965-6
1966	27		
1967	20		

*Note that in every year except two the gain from low to high was reduced by more than half in the following year.

Comparison Chart 4B
Zenith Radio

Year	Percent Increase Low to High Same Year	Percent Increase or Decrease of Low of First Year to Low of Following Year	
1956	33%	0%	1956-7
1957	33	33*	1957-8
1958	200	150*	1958-9
1959	130	50	1959-60
1960	46	7	1960-1
1961	156	31	1961-2
1962	81	24	1962-3
1963	62	19	1963-4
1964	42	0	1964-5
1965	97	48	1965-6
1966	93	5	1966-7
1967	50		

*Except for two years, the drop from the low of one year to the low of the following was at least half the rise from the low to high of the same year.

Summarizing the results of the first four tables, it can be concluded that regardless of how much these securities rose from the low to the high of the same year, they lost at least half the following year.

Low of One Year to High of the Following

The Low-High table reveals still another significant concept. There appears to be a substantial spread between the low of one year and the high reached the *following year.* This is contained in a fifth Low-High Spread chart. This time the dates are reversed, the earlier dates at the bottom followed by the succeeding years. This will be referred to as Chart 5.

Chart 5
Low-High Spread Chart
from Low of One Year
to High of Following Year
(Adjusted for splits and stock dividends)

	Standard Oil New Jersey			Zenith Radio		
Year	Lowest Price Per Share	Highest Price Per Share	Percent Spread	Lowest Price Per Share	Highest Price Per Share	Percent Spread
1967	$59	$71 ----- 7%		$48	$72 ---> 55%	
1966	66	84 --->13		46	89 --->186	
1965	74	90 ---> 20		31	61 ---> 97	
1964	75	93 --->58		31	44 ---> 69	
1963	58	77 ---> 71		26	42 --->100	
1962	45	60 ---> 46		21	38 --->136	
1961	41	52 ---> 37		16	41 ---> 174	
1960	38	51 ---> 11		15	22 --->120	
1959	46	59 ---> 23		10	23 ---> 470	
1958	48	60 ---> 25		4	12 --->200	
1957	48	69 ---> 38		3	4 ---> 33	
1956	50	63		3	4	

Chart 5 indicates the percentage spread between the low of one year to the high of the following year. For example, Standard Oil in 1957 had a 38% increase from $50, the low of 1956, to $69, the high for 1957, etc. Trace the "up" oblique lines for both securities, and the horizontal broken lines to the percentage spread.

It should be noted that the low of one year was always lower than the high of the following. This occurred in Standard Oil of New Jersey even during those years 1956-1961 when its market price was declining. *It seems that where a security is purchased at or near the low of one year, it should show a profit during the following year.*

This information is important only to those who, though they are not "in and outers," want to make capital gains regularly. There are times when they buy a security near the low of the year. However, peculiar adverse factors drive it lower after the purchase. Chart 5 indicates that it will probably rise during the following year and make a capital gain possible.

Future Predictions

The 5 charts contain a wealth of information, *to be studied and not merely read.* Charts 2-5 tell the same story in different ways. Essentially they say that most stocks go up—stop—and then drop, only to start the perennial cyclic pattern all over again. *The drop is normally more than half the rise.* This explains why securities that are bought after they have increased beyond the halfway mark usually result in losses, sometimes temporarily. The last 4 charts represent background information that should be recalled instantaneously when confronted with a "hot tip." This instantaneous recall should be as swift as the conditioned reflex that makes a person withdraw his hand when he accidentally touches a hot stove.

Chart 1 is the breadwinner. If understood properly and applied consistently it should increase the investor's annual yield substantially.

When to Start?

When is the best time to start a spread chart? Begin at the sound of a "tip" or "inside information." For example, start when told that an unusual earning report will soon be released or that a security will be "split." Instead of rushing to buy the stock make a Chart 1 analysis. The analysis may deter you from making a hasty and costly purchase.

A case in point is Pan American World Airways which split its stock two shares for one in May 1967. In January the stock hovered in the $55 range, down from its 1966 high of $79 a share. By April the security was climbing with great strength and vigor in anticipation of the great event. What should have been done? The first step would have been to make a spread chart which follows:

Year	Low	High	Percent Spread
1956	8	11	37
1957	6	10	67
1958	6	12	100
1959	10	18	80
1960	8	12	50
1961	8	12	50
1962	8	12	50
1963	11	27	146
1964	26	43	65
1965	25	56	124
1966	40	79	98
Actual 1967	55	74	37 (As of April)
Probable 1 (1967)	(55)	(83)	(50)
Probable 2 (1967)	(49)	(74)	(50)

The range of the stock since 1962 was from $8 to $79. The percent spread since 1956 varied from a low of 37% in 1956 to 146% in 1963. In April 1967, at $74 a share it was 37%. A realistic spread for the year should be at least 50%. In Probable 1 it was assumed that the low would hold and that the high would reach $83 a share. In Probable 2 it was assumed that the high of $74 would hold and the low would drop further to $49 a share. (See arithmetic at end of chapter.)

A price-earning ratio check (described in Chapter 3 and 4) was made which showed that the stock at $74 a share was selling at more than 20 times its three years' average earnings. This was much too high. The cautious approach was to assume that the high would not be pierced and the stock would drop below its existing low of $55 a share. We therefore discouraged the purchase. In August of 1967 the stock broke through its low. (The low for 1967 was $23 adjusted for the 2-to-1 split.)

If the analysis had been wrong, the stock would have climbed to approximately $83 a share. At $83 it would have been selling at a three-year price-earning ratio of 24 times, a very high rate.

This kind of analysis should be made before every purchase. Here are the circumstances under which it should be made.

1. Group doing well

An entire industrial group is doing well market-wise. The various tests described in subsequent chapters indicate that one or more members should be purchased. Here is a procedure that is recommended:

Make a Chart 1 spread test for each member of the group. If the group is doing well market-wise, the probability is that the lows of the year will hold. Assume a reasonable percentage spread from low to high of the same year based on past experience. Is there room for a substantial rise? If there is, make the additional tests suggested in future chapters, and buy the stock, if it meets the timing text of Chapter 2.

Example: Stock A, which is reasonably priced as determined by the tests, has a 10-year Chart 1 spread of from 30 to 65%. The range thus far has been this year 37 to 41 and the stock is currently selling at 39. Make the following chart:

	Year	Current Range		Percent Spread Low to High
Actual	1968	37	41	11
Probable 1	(1968)	(37)	(48)	(30)
Probable 2	(1968)	(31)	(41)	(30)

The actual spread, thus far, from low to high has been 11%. The spread has been at least 30% during the past decade. It is not unreasonable to assume that the spread will be at least 30% before the year ends. This will occur in one of three ways:

Condition 1. The low of 37 will hold, and the stock will pierce the high of 41 on the upside.

Condition 2. The high of 41 will not be pierced on the upside, but the low of 37 will drop further.

Condition 3. Both the low and the high will give way and thus establish the minimum 30% spread.

It is possible that this year's spread will be an exception to the previous pattern and will not be 30%. This anomaly is rare and will be ignored.

If Condition 1 prevails, and the low of 37 holds for the balance of the year, the high will be forced upward to 48. This figure is obtained by multiplying the low 37 by 130% or 1.30. This is indicated in Probable 1.

If Condition 2 prevails, and the high of 41 remains intact for the rest of the year, the low will have to drop to 31 to establish a 30% spread. The figure 31 is obtained by dividing the high of 41 by 130% or 1.30. This is indicated in Probable 2.

Condition 3 is not expected (at least not at this time) because the security selected is in a group that is doing well.

Summarizing the two possibilities:

	Year	Range This Year		Percentage Spread
1.	1968	37	48	30%
or				
2.	1968	31	41	30% (approx.)

Will it be 1 or 2? If our judgment is correct, and the group will continue to do well, the range will probably be 1, and the high reach at least $48 a share.

2. Group doing poorly

Even when a group is not doing well, it is possible to purchase a security near its lowest price of the year and let the normal Chart 1 spread yield a substantial profit.

First and foremost, all the checks that will be described in subsequent chapters should be made and the best securities selected, though they are doing poorly market-wise. Make a Chart 1 spread and note the normal range for the last 10 years. Assume it is from 30 to 65%. The stock is currently selling at $39 a share. This year's spread has been 37 to 41. The current spread is only 11%. It should be at least 30%. Either the stock will rise above $41 or the low of $37 will be pierced and it will plummet to $31 or lower. There is no need to hurry. Make a daily chart as described in Timing, Chapter 2, and watch the stock, each and every day. *You may have to wait months before making the purchase.* If the purchase is made at the right time, the rewards will be substantial and gratifying.

3. Stock doing badly

Hardly a day goes by without one or more securities making a low for the year. This calls for an immediate investigation. A spread chart should be made. If the percent spread, when the low is made, is substantially higher than the norm established during the last decade, it merits special attention, and daily watching, following the lines of Chapter 2.

A case in point is Insurance Company of North America, which is one of the finest in its industry. After reaching its high of $88¾ early in 1967 it began a significant descent reaching a low point of $52 a share in November 1967. This made the range to that date $52-88¾, a spread of 70%. In none of the previous 12 years was the spread as large. In 1958 it was $45-69, or 54%. In 1962 it was $66-107 or 62%. In one year, 1961, it was 48%, from $76 to 112.

Here is a Low-High Spread Chart of the company.

Insurance Company of North America
(Adjusted for splits and stock dividends)

Year	Low	High	Percent Increase
1956	41	52	27
1957	41	55	34
1958	45	69	54
1959	57	74	30
1960	60	79	32
1961	76	112	48
1962	66	107	62
1963	87	103	19
1964	86	100	35
1965	72	99	37
1966	68	91	34
1967	52	89	70

Because of the 70% spread from low to high the probability was that the security would not drop too significantly below $52. Inasmuch as the low was made in November, year-end tax selling was near its final phase. The procedure was to make a Chapter 2 chart, following the daily movement of the stock until the technical pattern indicated that the low would probably hold. That determined, the stock could be bought confidently.

Timing Is Important

Is the investor making his analysis during the first six months of the year or during the last six months?

If it is made during the early months, before earning reports have been published, many assumptions will have to be made. Will the economy do well? Will the industry do well? Which companies will be best?

If the stock has done well market-wise the previous year, the probability is there should be profit-taking. These securities should be avoided. On the other hand, there are usually many good quality securities that did poorly the previous year, closing near their lowest prices in December. They should be favored as candidates for purchase.

If the analysis is made during the second half of the year, the investor knows the percentage spread that has already been made. This should be quite helpful. In the case of Insurance Company of North America, just mentioned, a percentage spread of 70% had been made by November 1967 after a series of lows. The stock could have been purchased on this basis alone. This does not mean that the low for the year had been reached. End-of-year tax selling could depress it further. A daily chart should be made as described in Chapter 2. This will help determine when the selling pressure has been overbalanced by aggressive buying. This should pinpoint the price when the stock may be purchased with reasonable assurance that the low for the year had been established.

More Tests Ahead

While the spread chart is very important, it is only one of the tests that should be made. It may be considered an excellent "governor" reducing the risk factor.

The percentage spread varies considerably for each security. When making predictions for the probable lows and highs one should not be too rigid. They should serve as guides only, subject to market and economic conditions.

It should not be concluded that successful investing consists simply of making several charts and following a few rules mechanically. These were introduced as the *first* of a series of guidelines before investing. The charts should dissuade those who act hastily and repent slowly. They represent boundaries within which most securities move, some to high levels, others to lower ones. They are determined not so much by economic factors as by emotional ones. The economic forces determine the long-term trend of a security; the emotional ones, the perennial rhythmic "Yo-Yo" fluctuations. A governor or safety valve is necessary to prevent a "blowout." The Low-High charts perform that function.

The mathematics of probability applies to investments as it does to astronomy, physics, chemistry, insurance, and even psychology. If past patterns are applied to future situations the probability of their repetition is increased when the number of cases is large. Therefore, it should be applied to many securities, and not limited to a few.

Diversification of investments must or should be an essential part of our thinking. With all the care in the world, there will be anomalies here and there. However, if a great many securities are purchased as recommended in this book, the overall results should be good—in some cases, excellent.

Homework

One learns by doing. Making charts of every security owned provides good experience. More important, charts should be made of prospective purchases. This will provide valuable information, which will prevent hasty judgments.

Arithmetic

For those who have forgotten how to obtain percentage increase, this is a review.

Problem: What is the percent increase when a security rises from 21 to 38?

Step 1.   Subtract 21 from 38, or 38 − 21 equals 17.

Step 2.   Divide 17 by 21 or 17/21 equals .81 or 81%.

The division can be done easily by using a slide rule.

Summary of Chapter

Consistent profits result from logic, not luck. Pitfalls surround all investments. There are several guidelines that should be understood and followed. The first is to understand the fluctuation pattern of the security you plan to buy.

2
Timing

Each year, every security reaches a bottom. Each year every security reaches a top. Looking back at the record it seems easy to determine both. It is more difficult, perhaps impossible, to predict the future limits. In this chapter an attempt will be made to get as close as possible.

There are usually three periods when securities reach their lows:

1. There are a great many corporations whose earnings in any one year fall behind their previous year's figures. With few exceptions, their securities rise and fall, with the main trend on the downside. Those that do not recover during the first half of the year usually do poorly after July or August. In November and December, they are subjected to intense selling pressure by income-tax-minded individuals who engage in tax-loss selling.

Tax-loss selling should be thoroughly understood by investors and traders. For most people income from all sources starts on January 1st and ends on December 31st. Their taxes are based on income earned between these dates. During the latter half of the year they think of ways and means of reducing their income taxes for the year. One method is to sell those securities on which they have large losses. In this way they reduce profits they may have made during the year. Where they have no profits they take losses because they can reduce their earned income up to $1,000 for the year. If their losses are larger than

35

$1,000 they can apply the losses in excess of this amount to profits in future years or keep reducing their earned income by $1,000 a year.

Because of tax selling at the year end, it is a good season for buying depressed securities. December is particularly good. Although many beaten-down issues recover early in January, there are numerous opportunities in February when bargains are still available.

Special care should be exercised during November not to rush to buy. Sharp drops often occur when anxious sellers are so predominant they sacrifice their securities. The selling usually peters out in mid-December because those who own large blocks have completed their work and only small or sporadic activity continues to the end. There is usually a short period of recovery after Christmas.

2. Each year, almost without exception, there is at least one, often two "crises" when large selling waves take place. During these periods large blocks of securities, both good and bad, make lows for the year. It is of epidemic nature.

3. Every year some industrial groups do poorly financially; so do their securities. At one time it may be the drugs because of an investigation, or the steels, or chemicals, etc. During May and early June of 1967 the rubber stocks, which had been doing rather well, came in for selling and dropped to their lowest prices of the year. In December they rose to their highest prices.

Recognizing the normal pattern of securities, one should be alerted when certain stocks or groups start their annual descent. They should be followed closely while they drop until they "bottom" out. The objective is to buy them as close to that point as possible. The method which will now be discussed will be a combination of the Low-High Spread patterns of Chapter 1 and special charting.

A security in a declining episode normally drops for a period, recovers part of the loss, declines again, recovers, declines, etc., until it ultimately reaches a support level. The pattern of the decline appears like this:

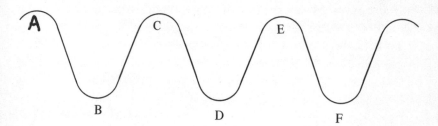

When the temporary recovery sets in, the temptation is to rush to buy before it is too late. To further confuse the matter the recovery is sometimes associated with large volume. There are many false starts. Great patience will be required to avoid making a premature commitment.

In studying the downtrend pattern, we found that the succeeding highs were usually lower than the previous one and the lows, lower. Thus C, E, etc., are successively lower. So, are D, F, etc. This trend may last a few weeks or many months. At times the decline is so long it exhausts one's patience. The investor is always afraid he will miss it. (There are times when he will. Most of the time he won't.)

In a broad and general way, we have found that points B, C, D, etc., follow the following general formula:

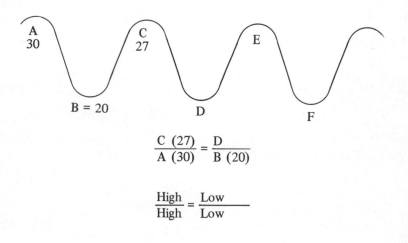

$$\frac{C\ (27)}{A\ (30)} = \frac{D}{B\ (20)}$$

$$\frac{High}{High} = \frac{Low}{Low}$$

D is found by cross-multiplying 27 and 20 and dividing by 30. D becomes 18.

To find the next crest E use the formula

$$\frac{D\ (18)}{B\ (20)} = \frac{E}{C\ (27)}$$

$$\frac{Low}{Low} = \frac{High}{High}$$

How can we recognize the recovery period? Tersely stated, the recovery normally takes place when the down chart described is replaced by another wherein each successive high is higher than the previous one and the successive lows are also higher than the preceding lows. The chart will then look like this:

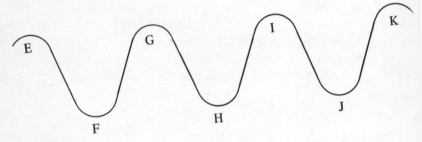

The points E, G, I, K, etc., can be determined approximately by a formula similar to the ones previously stated for the downturn.

The tops can be determined (approximately) as follows:

$$\frac{G}{F} = \frac{I}{H} \quad \text{or} \quad \frac{High}{Low} = \frac{High}{Low}$$

where I is the only number that is not known while the other three are known.

The values for the troughs F, H, J, etc., follow a similar formula:

$$\frac{I}{G} = \frac{J}{H} \qquad \frac{\text{High}}{\text{High}} = \frac{\text{Low}}{\text{Low}}$$

where J is unknown.

Before we examine specific examples, there are several generalizations:

1. Time moves very slowly before a trend is reversed. Exercise patience and restraint.

2. There are many false moves. In general, wait for at least two successive highs and lows before committing yourself.

3. Don't ignore the group. If the rest of the group is moving up while the security you are watching is moving down, and if the earnings are good, get in earlier rather than later. It may be the case of a fund or estate liquidating. The turnabout may be fast. If the entire group is moving down, especially if the interim reports are poor, don't rush. You may have a long wait. The point is, don't use the numbers mechanically. Here, as elsewhere, human judgment should not be subordinated to numbers. The latter are only guides.

4. When a security is moving up and the volume suddenly increases substantially, it is usually a sign that the move has reached its upper limit (possibly temporarily). This may surprise the reader who has been educated to think that strong volume on the upside is good. Experience does not support this. Where a company is being purchased by another, this may be an exception.

5. When the downtrend is nearing its end, the volume may increase with little or no motion, either way. It may be the signal that the support level is near at hand.

6. Near the end of the downtrend, the last gasps of the selling

may create a picture that looks like a W or series of W's. This may signify that there is support at the troughs. Thus:

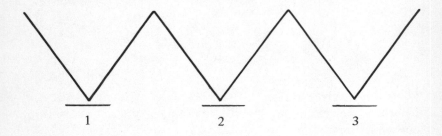

1, 2, 3 appear as support levels.

7. While you are preoccupied with the charting, don't ignore the p/e ratio. Move more slowly for the high p/e ratios; act more quickly for the low ones. The p/e ratios are of first importance, the charts second and not the other way round.

8. Finally: This method of charting is recommended only to determine *when the low of the year has probably* been reached. Warning: It is not recommended at other times. We are aware that some individuals use charts similar to these at any and all stages of a security's movement. We use it only to establish the low.

9. After the specific illustration we shall integrate this method of charting with the "spreads" of Chapter 1.

Monsanto Chemical

The following discussion will be limited to the movement of Monsanto Chemical during 1966 and early 1967. This "blue chip" chemical normally sold at a 3-year p/e ratio in the high twenties. Because of difficulties in 1966, especially in its fiber products, earnings fell. So did the stock.

Here are the earnings and range of the stock for the past decade:

Monsanto Chemical
Earnings and Range
1956-1966

Earnings Per Share	Years	Low	High	Percent Spread Low to High
$1.51	1956	$27	$42	57%
1.43	1957	25	35	40
1.32	1958	26	35	35
2.44	1959	33	49	48
2.22	1960	30	49	63
2.22	1961	39	52	34
2.50	1962	32	48	50
2.61	1963	45	61	35
3.58	1964	58	83	43
3.81	1965	76	91	19
3.48	1966	38	83	130

Squared paper is recommended for the study. The first column contains the date, the second the price and the third the volume. Once we became interested in the security, this information was recorded daily. Prior to that we recorded only prices weekly.

On or about June 23, 1966, we noted that the price had fallen to $67 per share, down from its 1965 high of $91. We went back to January 7, 1966, and recorded the high and low weekly figures that appeared significant (see page 42).

Discussion

On January 7, 1966, Monsanto closed at $82¾. By March 31st it had fallen to $77⅛ The ellipse around the figure signifies that this price represents a low for the movement. By April 14th it recovered to $78⅝. The box around a figure indicates a high for the movement. The low on June 23rd was *lower* than the previous low of March 31st. The high on June 24th was

Date	Price	Volume		Date	Price	Volume		Date	Price	Volume
1/7	82 3/4		→	3/31	77 1/8		→	4/14	78 5/8	
6/23	66 5/8	9000	→	6/24	67 1/8	7800	→	6/27	66 5/8	4800
6/28	66 3/4	11600	→	6/29	66 5/8	7100	→	6/30	66	26400
7/1	65 7/8	9700	→	7/5	65 5/8	10400	→	7/6	65 1/2	25200
7/7	65 1/4	18800	→	7/8	65 1/2	9200				

lower than the previous high on April 14th.

Thereafter the security moved lower. The volume increased significantly on the downside on June 30th, driving the stock down to $65¼ by July 7th and 11th.

At this price the security was lower than it was at the previous low of June 23rd. A correction took place for the next few weeks that lifted the security to a high of $68⅜ by July 25th. This was higher than it was at its previous high of $68⅛ reached on June 24th.

Following this hopeful move the price retreated to $64 by August 4th. The next day it rose sharply to $67⅛ on increased volume.

Prices kept moving lower and lower with temporary increases. The pattern was typical of bear markets. Each successive high was lower than the previous one. Each successive low was likewise lower than the previous lows. The September 14th recovery to $58¾ fell short of the previous high of July 25th or the intermediate highs since then.

During September and early October the trend was decisively on the downside with few sparks of hope.

Date	Price	Volume		Date	Price	Volume		Date	Price	Volume
7/11	(65 1/4)	12700	→	7/12	65 5/8	10900	→	7/13	65 7/8	21000
7/14	67 1/2	12800	→	7/15	67 5/8	10400	→	7/18	67 1/8	15200
7/19	67 3/4	16200	→	7/20	67 5/8	12800	→	7/21	68	10400
7/22	68	12500	→	7/25	68 3/8	12700	→	7/26	67 1/8	11500
7/27	67	15200	→	7/28	66 1/8	12400	→	7/29	65 3/4	12000
8/1	64 3/4	11600	→	8/2	64 1/2	9100	→	8/3	64 5/8	9600
8/4	(64)	9100	→	8/5	67 1/8	12400				

During the latter days of October significant support came in and the highs of October 25th and October 28th had all the earmarks of the beginning of a recovery.

It is usually best to wait after a recovery until the next bottom to see if the low of $41⅝ on October 26th would hold. It did not and the security dropped to $39¼ before turning up to its next temporary high of $41½ on November 16th. Thereafter, for the remainder of November the stock moved within a narrow range signifying that the tax selling could not depress the security further. Even though the up-pattern had not been established, the security could have been purchased near the $40 area. One could expect additional income tax selling until the middle of December. There is little point in waiting when it appears that a support level has been reached.

Date	Price	Volume		Date	Price	Volume		Date	Price	Volume
8/8	66 1/2	7200	→	8/9	65 1/2	6000	→	8/10	64 1/2	6000
8/11	64 3/8	9700	→	8/12	63 7/8	11800	→	8/15	61 5/8	5800
8/16	(60 3/8)	12300	→	8/17	60 1/2	12700	→	8/18	60 1/2	10600
8/19	61 3/4	13100	→	8/22	60 5/8	10900	→	8/23	(60 3/8)	18300
8/24	61 7/8	9700	→	8/25	60 5/8	8900	→	8/26	60 1/2	10800
8/29	58 5/8	17900	→	8/30	58 3/4	32000	→	8/31	57 5/8	11400
9/1	56 1/2	15500	→	9/2	57 1/2	7200	→	9/6	(55 5/8)	9700
9/7	55 7/8	7700	→	9/8	56 7/8	21600	→	9/9	56 3/4	14100
9/12	58	18100	→	9/13	58 5/8	17100	→	9/14	58 6/8	11200
9/15	57	12700	→	9/16	55 7/8	34400	→	9/19	55 1/8	18200
9/20	53 5/8	13200	→	9/21	50 5/8	28800	→	9/22	51 1/4	
9/23	49 3/4	10400	→	9/26	49	19600	→	9/27	49	20600

Date	Price	Volume		Date	Price	Volume		Date	Price	Volume
9/28	48 7/8	10100	→	9/29	47 1/4		→	9/30	45 7/8	31500
10/3	44	19300	→	10/4	44 1/2	24000	→	10/5	43 5/8	13200
10/6	43 1/4	16500	→	10/7	(40 3/4)	21800	→	10/10	41 7/8	21600
10/11	41 1/2	24800	→	10/12	41 1/2	16800	→	10/13	39 1/2	
10/14	(39 3/8)	44200	→	10/17	40 1/8	32300	→	10/18	40 1/4	30400
10/19	(39)	21300	→	10/20	39 1/4	21300	→	10/21	40	
10/24	40 3/4	9700	→	10/25	42 3/8	12800	→	10/26	(41 5/8)	30700

Date	Price	Volume		Date	Price	Volume		Date	Price	Volume
10/27	41 3/4	29600	→	10/28	43 1/8	22800	→	10/31	42 5/8	51700
11/1	41 7/8	16300	→	11/2	41 5/8	25600	→	11/3	41 1/2	16100
11/4	41 1/2	18100	→	11/7	40 1/2	24500	→	11/9	(39 1/4)	29800
11/10	40 1/8	24100	→	11/11	40 7/8		→	11/14	40	55300
11/15	41 1/4	25700	→	11/16	41 1/2	43200	→	11/17	40 7/8	24400

11/18	40 1/8	34300	→	11/21	39 7/8	37900	→	11/22	39 3/8	27000
11/23	(38 3/4)	25700	→	11/24	[40]	20500	→	11/28	39 1/2	33000
11/29	39 1/4	32500	→	11/30	(39 1/4)	17500				

Date	Price	Volume		Date	Price	Volume		Date	Price	Volume
12/1	39 3/8	25700	→	12/2	39 5/8	27300	→	12/5	40	20400
12/6	40 1/2	41500	→	12/7	41 1/2	283000	→	12/8	43 1/8	126700
12/9	[44 1/2]	91800	→	12/12	44	68200	→	12/13	(42 5/8)	55700
12/14	42 3/4	32300	→	12/15	43 3/8	29200	→	12/16	[43 5/8]	28600
12/19	43 1/2	25800	→	12/20	42 7/8	29800	→	12/21	42 1/2	30200
12/22	42 3/8	28700	→	12/23	42 3/8	26900	→	12/27	41 3/4	22900
12/28	41 3/8	23800	→	12/29	41	23700	→	12/30	41 1/4	29700

The early days of December witnessed a significant recovery. The volume on December 7th and 8th was substantial and confirmed support.

The high of December 9th was higher than the previous high of $41½ on November 16th. The low of December 13th was higher than the preceding low of $38¾ of November 23rd. The probability is that a new pattern has been established.

More important than the pattern is the probability that the low of 1966 had been established at or near $40.

Emphasizing the statement made previously in this chapter *the best time to purchase a security is near the end of the year, when one can be certain of the low of the year.* The spreads of Chapter 1 can be counted on to operate the following year.

Summary of Discussion of Monsanto Chemical

Monsanto, an excellent quality security, suffered its worst market break in recent years. Once the downtrend started it continued to the very end of November. The chart pattern was classic. There were false upturns which failed to materialize.

Its drop during the second half of the year was also classic. Tax selling started early and continued to the very end. Those who waited patiently to the end of November were rewarded. *Regardless of pattern, late November and early December are good periods to buy depressed securities.*

Spread Chart of R. H. Macy 1957 to 1966

Year	Lowest Price Per Share	Highest Price Per Share	Percent Spread L & H
1957	$14	$16	14
1958	14	20	43
1959	19	22	16
1960	19	24	26
1961	22	37	68
1962	23	36	47
1963	28	38	36
1964	37	50	35
1965	45	60	33
1966	43	55	28

R. H. Macy

The movement of R. H. Macy during the early months of 1967 represents a more classic picture of timing than did Monsanto Chemical. The Chapter 1 spread chart of Macy for the past decade is above.

Discussion

The first two weeks of January saw Macy hover near the lows made in December of the previous year.

On January 5th it made its low of 1967 and continued making lows on January 12th and 13th.

Date	Price	Volume		Date	Price	Volume		Date	Price	Volume
1/3	42 3/8	400	→	1/4	42 3/4	1100	→	1/5	42 1/4	2100
1/6	42 1/4	1200	→	1/9	42 5/8	800	→	1/10	42 3/4	1400
1/11	42 1/2	1100	→	1/12	42 1/8	2300	→	1/13	41 3/4	13X P/E Ratio

It looked as if this security was destined for lower prices despite its modest 3-year p/e ratio of 13x.

Note

It is a good idea to place a small L (in red) in the box when a low is made.

The downtrend continued for two more days until January 17th when the stock closed at $41½. Thereafter it rose easily with negligible volume to a high of $43 ⅞ on January 25th. The previous high had been made on December 27, 1966, when the stock closed at $43¼. Following the high on January 25th. The stock moved off for a few days to a low of $43⅛ on January 30th and 31st. This was higher than the previous lows of

Date	Price	Volume		Date	Price	Volume		Date	Price	Volume
1/16	(41 1/2)	1700	→	1/17	41 1/2	3000	→	1/18	41 3/4	3900
1/19	41 5/8	3700	→	1/20	42 3/8	3200	→	1/23	42 1/2	4000
1/24	43 3/8	2200	→	1/25	43 7/8	1500	→	1/26	43	1500
1/27	43 1/4	2100	→	1/30	(43 1/8)	900	→	1/31	43 1/8	1100
2/1	43 3/8	1000	→	2/2	43 1/2	1600	→	2/3	44 1/2	2200
2/6	45 1/2	5500	→	2/7	45 3/8	900	→	2/8	(44 3/8)	1300
2/9	44 1/2	3300	→	2/10	46 1/2	73600	→	2/13	47	2400

January 16th and 17th. It turned about to move upward to $45½ on February 6th. This was higher than the previous high of January 25th.

It dropped to $44⅜ for a low on February 8th, and then turned about and began rising again. At that point it was reasonably clear that the *low* for 1967 had probably been reached.

Again, the objective is to ascertain with reasonable certainty that the low of the year has been established. When the security reached approximately $45 a share an important decision had to be reached. The low for 1967 was $41 and the high at that point $45. The low-high spread at that point was not quite 10%. A reasonable minimum low-high spread should be at least 30%. (See page 47.)

There were two possibilities: Either the 1967 low of $41 would hold and a high, at least 30% above it, established, or $45 would be the high of 1967 and the low of $41 would drop further.

Let us reconstruct the two alternatives for 1967:

	Low	High	Low-High Spread
Probable 1.	$41	$53	30%
Probable 2.	35	45	30

In other words, either the security would fall to approximately $35 a share or it would rise to at least $53 a share.

Hindsight makes the solution easy; foresight difficult. In the case of Macy, the graphic pattern suggested that the low had probably been established. The p/e ratio at $45 was 14x, which was modest in its group. Finally, the first quarter report of the company that ended in October was $.93 vs $.80 for the same period of last year. All this reasoning lead to the conclusion that the $41 low would probably hold and the security would rise to at least $53 per share. The security rose to $77⅜ during 1967 after splitting two for one.

This discussion is intended as a guide for the investor. He should consider the following factors before making the decision to buy or wait:

1. Does the chart suggest that the low for the year has probably been established?

2. Using the low-high percentage spreads, what are the two alternatives?

3. Where is the p/e ratio of the stock relative to its group?

4. Do the year's earnings appear to be better, worse, or the same as that of the previous year?

Conclusion

Timing at best is difficult. It should be approached with the same care that should be given to quality and p/e ratio. Even then, errors will be made. However, if every security is purchased with the care that is suggested, the probability is that the overall results will be satisfactory.

3

Comparison Shopping

The method used most often by those who buy securities is not sound investment. They buy a stock glamorized either by an exciting press story or friend. Rarely do they study the company's record or its stock market performance.

This method is basically unsound. The "tip" or inside story is often misleading. The expected merger or stock split may not take place. The larger anticipated profits may not mean an increase in the market price of the stock, which has already increased substantially. Quite often a security drops in price after the "good" news has been published.

There are many cautious investors who buy good securities whose future earnings appear promising. Even this method has its shortcomings. If they are purchased without regard to the "Spread Theory" of Chapter 1 and "Timing" of Chapter 2, they may result in losses or lower profits.

The recommended method is comparison shopping. This is standard procedure in business and with wise shoppers. It is logical and capable of mathematical analysis.

Successful investing consists of selecting the right securities, rejecting the wrong ones and timing the purchases and sales correctly. This chapter deals with the selection and rejection of securities on the basis of an analysis as specific as "spread" and "timing."

Comparison Shopping,

How does one go about comparison shopping. Can U.S. Steel be compared with I.B.M.? It cannot because they are in different industries. Securities in the same or closely related industries can be compared. For example, U.S. Steel and Bethlehem Steel; Standard Oil of New Jersey and the Texas Company; Monsanto Chemical and Olin Mathieson, etc. can be compared. Their sales and profit growth can be placed alongside one another and be compared. Their market price can be measured in terms of their profits and the better value should emerge.

By way of example, consider two companies in the same industry, whose growth records are similar. The first earns $2 a share and sells for $30. The second earns $3 a share and sells for $33. It is quite obvious that the second security is a better value. What is needed is a measuring device that will select it quickly. There is such a yardstick. It is called the price-earning ratio or p/e ratio. (Earnings can be obtained from Standard & Poor's Reports).

The Price Earning Ratio (P/E)

The p/e ratio indicates the number of dollars at which a stock is selling *for each dollar of earnings.* For example, if the earnings are $2 a share and the market price is $30, the p/e ratio is 15. It means that the stock is selling at $15 for each dollar of earnings. In the second example the earnings are $3 a share, the selling price is $33 and the p/e ratio is 11. The p/e ratio is obtained by dividing the market price of a stock by its earnings. (A slide rule is quite helpful in determining the p/e ratio.)

Earnings

This obvious question is difficult to answer. Shall we take current earnings or, as some do, next year's? Neither should be taken. Profits of most industrials vary widely from year to year. They are up one year and down the following. Experience shows it is desirable to take the average of the last three years.

This will include good, bad and normal years. By way of example, if the annual earnings are $2, $3, and $2.80 the average is obtained by adding the three to get $7.80 and dividing the sum by 3. This results in a profit average of $2.60 per share. An exception might be public utilities whose profits are stable, so that current earnings may be used.

Examples of p/e ratio

Before discussing the importance of the p/e ratio, the reader should become familiar with the method and meaning. Here are several examples. Determine the p/e ratio in each case and compare your answer with the one in the last column.

Market Price	Earnings (Average last 3 years)	Price-Earning Ratio
$33	$3	11
45	5	9
32	2	16
29	1.85	15.7
34	2.38	14.3
55	3.71	14.8
46 1/2	2.63	17.7

The p/e ratio provides the investor with several safeguards to guide him.

Safeguard No. 1—P/E Ratio and Yield Are Inversely Related

The first safeguard that the p/e ratio performs is to warn the buyer that the higher the ratio rises the lower will be the yield that is returned on the investment. Most companies distribute approximately half their earnings to their stockholders as dividends and retain the remainder for future expansion. A company that earns $2 a share and whose stock is selling at $20 has a p/e ratio of 10. If this company pays a dividend of $1 per share, the yield is 5%. If the same stock becomes popular and rises to $40, the p/e ratio increases to 20. The dividend is still

$1 per share, so the yield is now only 2½%. Here are a few examples of earnings, p/e ratios, dividends and yields. The reader should check each.

Price-Earning Ratio and Yield Are Inversely Related

Price of Stock	Average Earnings	Price-Earning Ratio (P/E Ratio)	Dividends (1/2 of earnings)	Yield
$20	$2	10	$1.00	5.0%
36	3	12	1.50	4.2
56	4	14	2.00	3.6
24	1.50	16	.75	3.1
30	.75	40	.38	1.3

Note that as the p/e ratio rises the yield falls. Why do people buy high p/e ratio stocks? It's a case of "hope springs eternal." They hope that the company's earnings and dividends will rise in the future. It represents sacrificing current income for long term capital gains. In some instances the rewards are significant; in many cases the losses are greater than the hoped-for gains.

The "Has-Been Growth Stocks"

Currently I.B.M., Syntex, Xerox are today's favored growth stocks. The past had its favorites, too. Unfortunately, their golden era is behind them. As of April 1967, many former glamour stocks were selling at half or less their highest price during the last decade. At the top of the facing page is a very small sampling of securities listed on the New York Stock Exchange which start with the letter A.

There are undoubtedly hundreds of such securities listed on the New York Stock Exchange. If the list included stocks on the American Exchange and those that are unlisted, the total would easily exceed the thousand mark. Here is a research project for a doctorate thesis. It might result in an organization which could qualify for "Growth Seekers Anonymous."

A Sampling of Fallen Heroes of the Past Decade

Security	Approximate Market Price April 1967	Highest Price Past Decade	Date of Highest Price
Addressograph-Multigraph	$50	$109	1961
Admiral Corp.	28	67	1966
Alberto-Culver Co.	23	42	1963
Allied Products	37	71	1966
American Machine and Foundry	18	64	1961
American Photo Copy	8	46	1961

Spotting the High Ones

The p/e ratio yardstick spots these hopefuls easily. They are betrayed by their high multiples. Note their p/e ratios and yields.

P/E Ratios and Yields of Past Heroes on the New York Stock Exchange

Security	Highest Price and Year		Average Earnings Previous 3 Years	P/E Ratio	Dividend	Yield
Addressograph-Multigraph	$109	(1961)	$1.67	65x	$.90	.8 of 1%
Admiral	67	(1966)	.92	73x	.38	.6 of 1
Alberto-Culver	42	(1964)	.41	102x	.18	.4 of 1
Allied Products	70 1/2	(1966)	.92	77x	.50	.7 of 1
American Machine and Foundry	64	(1961)	1.22	53x	.88	1.4
American Photocopy	46	(1961)	.45	102x	.29	.6 of 1

The high p/e ratios and low yields are quite pronounced. For example, Alberto-Culver sold as high as $42 in 1964. Its 3-year p/e ratio was 102 and it yielded .4 of 1% of this price. In the case of Addressograph-Multigraph the p/e ratio was 65 and its yield .8 of 1%. This is the story of the others in the list and countless hundreds or thousands similarly priced. Is there any wonder that more than a million and half people lost 4 billion dollars in 1963?

Safeguard No. 2—The Sound Is Deafening

The p/e ratio is equipped with an electronic bell that starts ringing when it crosses the 15x barrier and increases in crescendo as the multiple rises. When it crosses the 50x mark the sound is deafening, but only to those whose ears are attuned to it. The others go blithely on their way, hearing nothing and seeing nothing, until lightning strikes. Then they complain that the other person has all the luck.

Ratios under 10 are usually quite safe, unless something is drastically wrong with the company or industry. Even in a laggard group, whose earnings are stable and which has little growth, the "spreads" of Chapter 1 help the investor to his profits. While waiting anxiously he is usually getting 5% return on his investment. In the end he does quite well. As the ratios rise, the yields drop and the risks start increasing. When 15x is reached the time has come for a critical appraisal. The rose-colored glasses should be removed and the situation viewed realistically. The yield on a security at 15x will usually be approximately 3% annually. This is low and will require considerable capital gains to compensate for the meager yield. Above 15x the risk increases sharply, especially for most securities.

The market price at which a security sells is part economic and part emotion. It is the latter that accounts for the perennial fluctuations. It's a kind of manic-depressive cycle. This explains why a security can at one time sell at $109 per share and a few years later fall to $35 (U.S. Steel). When it was selling at $109 a share its p/e ratio was 18. At $35 its p/e was 9. Recognizing this, it is important to be alert to avoid the security when hysteria takes command, and buy it when nobody wants it.

Examine the p/e ratios and yields of three representative steel stocks in 1959 and 1967.

Representative Steel Stocks in 1959
(Adjusted for stock dividends and splits)

Name of Stock	Highest Price	3-Year P/E Ratio	Dividend	Yield
Bethlehem Steel	$ 59	16	$2.40	4.0%
Republic Steel	82	16	3.00	3.7
U.S. Steel	109	18	3.00	2.8

Here are the same securities in April of 1967:

Representative Steel Stocks in 1967

Name of Stock	Price April 1967	3-Year P/E Ratio	Dividend	Yield
Bethlehem Steel	$ 37	11	$1.80	4.9%
Republic Steel	49	9.5	2.00	4.1
U.S. Steel	47	11	2.00	4.3

Steels were in fashion in 1959, but out of style by early 1967. No doubt they will return to favor at some future time.

The action of the steel group is no exception. Consider the domestic and international oils. A few years ago the domestics were in disfavor while the internationals were in fashion. At that time the domestics sold at relatively low p/e ratios of 12x or 13x. However, the internationals were selling as high as 18x or 19x. All this has changed. In 1967 the domestics were selling at the higher p/e ratios while the internationals were in the lower range. Another example can be found in the chemicals. Not so long ago they were at the very height of their popularity, selling at p/e ratios in the high twenties. In 1957 they had fallen to the point where one of their finest could be bought as low as 12x (Monsanto).

The p/e ratio not only sounds a warning as prices rise, it

predicts disaster when the infection is of epidemic proportion. When a few securities sell out of line an orderly correction takes place. However, when the number becomes vast the entire market is endangered. This happened in 1929, 1937, 1946 and 1962. Bear markets are caused by previous excesses.

Safeguard No. 3—Buy the Lowest P/E Ratio

One of the most important attributes of the p/e ratio is its ability to select the best buy in an industrial group. The method is to line the prospective candidates alongside each other, with their prices, earnings and p/e ratios. Select the one with the lowest p/e ratio and subject it to a series of tests including the "spread" tests of Chapter 1.

Consider a few examples to illustrate the method.

Monsanto Chemical vs. Olin Mathieson

Here are two important chemical companies. Monsanto has been the favorite for many years with Olin Mathieson lagging behind in public favor. However, the tables were turned in 1966-67. Olin Mathieson became the favorite while Monsanto dragged behind. Here are the two securities in September 1964 and then again in April 1967:

**Comparison of Monsanto Chemical and Olin Mathieson
on September 16, 1964**

Security	Price	3-Year P/E Ratio
Monsanto Chemical	$86	25x
Olin Mathieson	52	17x

**Comparison of Monsanto Chemical and Olin Mathieson
in April 1967**

Security	Price	P/E Ratio
Monsanto Chemical	$47	13
Olin Mathieson	70	18

The turnabout is too bizarre to believe. Olin Mathieson has been the "bridesmaid" but never the "bride" while Monsanto Chemical was mentioned in hushed tones. The miracle occurred in 1966-67 when they changed places. Does this mean that a new era is at hand? We doubt it. It is our opinion that Monsanto Chemical is now the better value.

Although only two chemicals were selected as examples of the method, a list of all chemicals should be made. After making a basic comparison, which will be described in Chapter 4, the p/e ratio should be obtained of those that qualify. The security with the lowest p/e ratio should be selected, subject to the spread tests of Chapter 1. The latter is quite important because even the security with the lowest p/e ratio will be subject to the perennial bouncing even while it is making its ascending move.

When should a security be sold? In general, it should be sold, if (1) it is selling at the highest p/e ratio in its group; (2) if, in addition, its Chapter 1 spread indicates that it has increased beyond the norm; (3) if it has been replaced in the p/e ratio rank by an equally good security in its industry, or in some other important industry.

There are many investors who rarely sell for a multitude of reasons. They buy and hold. They bypass the peaks and troughs and enjoy the long-term trend. There is much merit to this method, if the owner does not need the additional income. It results in a relaxed, possibly longer life. It is preferred to the in and-out trader, who lives in pent-up excitation, his blood pressure throbbing.

Summary of Chapter

Securities should be purchased in the accepted business method of comparison shopping. This requires studying an industrial group, rather than a single security. The yardstick that is used is the p/e ratio. This determines the number of dollars one pays for each dollar of earnings.

There are four safeguards inherent in the p/e ratio:

1. The p/e ratio warns that the higher the ratio the lower will be the yield on the investment.

2. When the p/e ratio rises above 15x the danger zone is reached. There are some securities that have crossed this threshold safely. A great many are like meteors that burn brightly but not long enough.

3. The p/e ratio searches each industrial group and selects the most neglected security. If this one satisfies other requirements it becomes worthy of purchase.

4. Finally, when the p/e ratios of too many securities have crossed beyond the danger zone, the correction turns epidemic and a bear market follows. This is what happened during the years 1929, 1937, 1946 and 1962.

4
Buy Low—Sell High

At some time in their history most securities enjoy being popular with the investing and speculative public. Then the wind changes and with it public support. When they are favored they possess all the virtues. The management is brilliant, the future promising, and the sponsorship limitless. Then, all of a sudden, everything goes wrong. Fierce competition sets in. Their officers are old men and their future is threatened by a black cloud. At one time they sell at high p/e ratios and at another at low ones.

It is the intent of this chapter to present the case for buying good, sound securities when they are at their low p/e ratio phase and sell them when they have been lifted beyond reasonable heights. We shall give several examples, which are representative.

Example 1. Carrier vs. Trane Co.

Carrier and Trane are both important companies in the air-conditioning field. Both have had consistently good earning records. However, Trane has been the undisputed leader with the investing public. As a result it has sold at a higher p/e ratio than Carrier. Let us start our analysis in July 1964 when Carrier sold at a 3-year p/e ratio of 16.5 while Trane sold at a multiple of 27. Carrier sold at approximately $55 and Trane at $48 per share. Since then, both securities have done well. Carrier split its stock three for two in 1965.

The scene shifts to May 16, 1967, the date this chapter is being written. Carrier is selling for $57½ per share or $86¼ on the original stock. Trane is $60 a share. Thus, in a period of not quite 3 years the market price of the lower p/e ratio security (Carrier) increased 56% while the price of the higher p/e ratio security (Trane) increased 25% from $48 to $60.

The following table describes the change:

Changes in Prices and P/E Ratio of Carrier and Trane

	July 1964		May 16, 1967		
Security	Approxi-mate Price July 1964	3-Year P/E Ratio	Closing Price May 16, 1967	3-Year P/E Ratio May 16, 1967	Percent Increase
Carrier Corp.	$55	16.5	$86 1/4*	21.4	56
Trane Co.	48	27	60	26	25

*Priced to reflect 3/2 split.

Example 2 Ford vs. General Motors

Here are two companies with similar operations. Both have maintained their share of the auto market and have done well. However, General Motors has consistently sold at a higher p/e ratio than Ford. As in the previous example, go back to July 1964 when Ford sold at approximately $52 and General Motors at $97 a share. Their 3-year p/e ratios were Ford 11x and General Motors 16.5x.

Both securities moved up and down for the next two and half years, which brings them to May 16, 1967. At the close of that day Ford sold at $52½ while General Motors was $82. At the end of almost 3 years Ford stood still while General Motors dropped 15% from $97 to $82 a share. At this point General Motors was still selling at a higher p/e ratio than Ford, but as in the case of Carrier vs. Trane, the gap had narrowed.

The following table describes the changes:

Changes in Prices and P/E Ratios of General Motors and Ford

Security	Approximate Price July 1964	3-Year P/E Ratio	Closing Price May 16, 1967	3-Year P/E Ratio May 16, 1967	Percent Increase (Decrease)
Ford	$52	11	$52 1/2	9.5	0
General Motors	97	16.5	82	12.6	(15)

Example 3. Comparison of Four Banks

The next example will be four banks that are listed on the New York Stock Exchange. Their overall operations are comparable so that they are similarly affected by economic conditions. In July 1964 they were selling at different p/e ratios; the highest at 20x and the lowest at 14.5x. As in the previous examples time marched on and corrected the disparities. The following table describes the changes.

Changes of Prices and P/E Ratio of 4 Banks Listed on N.Y.S.E.

	July 1964		May 16, 1967		
Security	Approximate Price July 1964	3-Year P/E Ratio	Closing Price May 16, 1967	3-Year P/E Ratio May 16, 1967	Percent Increase (Decrease)
Northwest Bancorp.	$46	14.5	$52 1/2	13.5	14
Marine Midland	31 1/2	15.5	29 5/8	12	(6)
Chase Manhattan	66	16.5	61 1/2	14	(7)
Western Bancorp.	36	20	31 3/8	15.5	(13)

This table suggests many interesting conclusions. First, the only stock that appreciated during the 3-year period was Northwest Bancorp. which was selling at the lowest p/e ratio in 1964. Second, the stock that suffered the largest drop was Western Bancorp. which was selling at the highest p/e ratio. Third, the group as a whole enjoyed greater public support back in 1964 than it did in 1967. In the former period the p/e ratios were higher than they were in the latter. The reversal may have resulted from the tight money market of 1966 which adversely affected bank securities.

These three examples could be repeated for chemicals, drugs, oils, rubber, steel, copper, utilities, rails, etc., wherever corporations operate on a comparable basis. In the vast majority of cases the results will be similar to the illustrations. Undoubtedly, there will be exceptions.

This type of analysis is difficult for the computer and electronic industries where earnings are not comparable. These are the high p/e ratio "growth" securities with their risks and rewards. Good common sense that weighs risk and reward will have to guide the investor.

P/E Ratios of Three Oils

As a climax to this discussion we should like to present the result of a 16-year continuous study that we made of the movement of three large domestic and international oils from 1951 to 1967. They are the Standard Oil of California, Standard Oil of New Jersey and The Texas Company.

Our study started in January 1951, when all three were selling at approximately the same 3-year p/e ratio of 8. For the next 8 weeks The Texas Company took the lead. In the middle of February Standard Oil of New Jersey replaced it and held it for the balance of the year.

Here is a chart of the p/e ratios of the three companies for 1951:

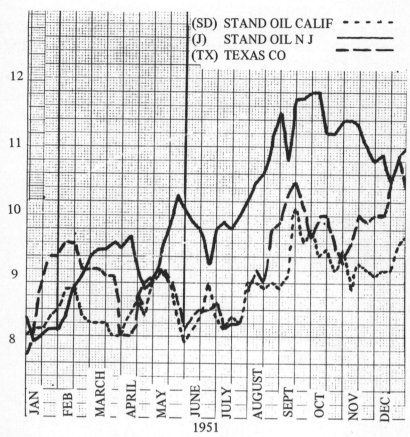

Trace the movements slowly and note how many times the lines representing the three companies cross. For example, *on or about April 15th, they "knotted." This means that they were all selling at the same p/e ratio.* Standard Oil of New Jersey and The Texas Company which had been selling at higher p/e ratios previously dropped, while Standard Oil of California, which had been the laggard, rose. Note that prior to February Standard Oil of New Jersey trailed behind for a month and a half. After April 15th, Standard Oil of California and The Texas Company moved along harmoniously, crossing each other many times.

In 1952 Standard Oil of New Jersey took a decisive lead, selling at approximately 13x earnings while the other two sold near the 10x level. For the greater part of the year Standard Oil of California sold in second place while The Texas Company trailed. The group as a whole did not do well that year, the biggest loser being Standard Oil of New Jersey. At the close of the year Standard Oil of California took the lead, with Jersey in second place and The Texas Company last. Here is a chart of 1952:

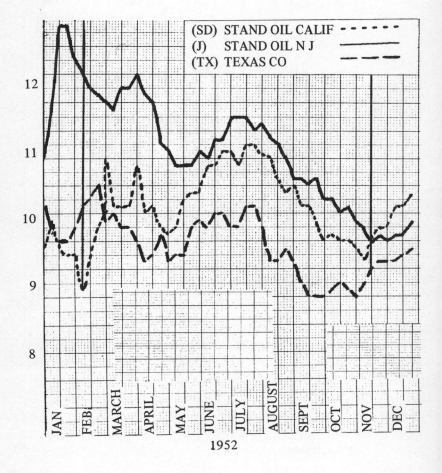

During the ensuing years the three moved about, the lead changing continuously. In the latter part of 1955 and through all of 1956 Standard Oil of New Jersey was in front, with the other two intertwining. Thereafter Standard Oil of New Jersey and The Texas Company fought each other for first place while Standard Oil of California trailed. In 1967 The Texas Company was clearly in front with Jersey second and California last. However, the difference between the latter two was not too significant. Here is a chart for 1967:

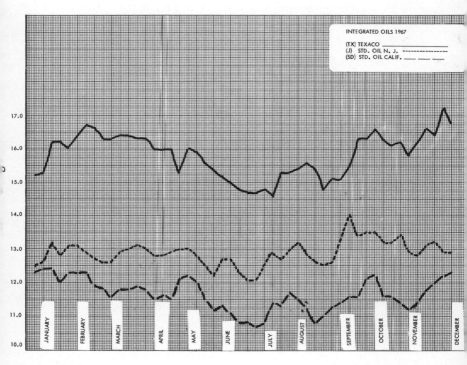

1967

There are two significant conclusions that can be deduced from this long-term study.

1. In the main the lowest p/e ratio represented the best value. In good markets it rose more than the others and in bad markets fell least.

2. There were times when the group enjoyed investor confidence and sold as high as 20x their 3-year earnings. There were other times when they sold as low as 8x.

Procedure

The following is a suggested procedure for those who want to start their own continuous study of homogeneous groups.

The first step is to make a list of companies that operate in the same or in comparable fields. After making certain that their overall earning and structural pattern is similar (see Chapter 5), they should be listed one beneath the other with the following background information. Earnings for the last three years, and the average, the price of the stock each week or month, depending on the time that the investor can allot to this work. The p/e ratio. Here is a typical example involving Ford, Chrysler and General Motors:

Date (1967)	4/27	5/4	5/11	5/18
Ford (price)	54 1/4	54 3/4	54 3/8	51 3/8
P/E ratio	10	10	10	9.3
Earnings and average	4.56 (1964)	6.33 (1965)	5.63 (1966)	Avg. 5.51
General Motors (price)	84 3/4	84 3/8	83 1/4	80
P/E ratio	13	13	12.8	12.3
Earnings and average	6.05 (1964)	7.40 (1965)	6.24 (1966)	Avg. 6.56
Chrysler (price)	43 7/8	45 1/8	43 1/2	43 5/8
P/E ratio	9.3	9.6	9.3	9.3
Earnings and average	5.46 (1964)	5.16 (1965)	4.16 (1966)	Avg. 4.93

Explanation of chart

The use of columnar paper is advised. Each security requires three lines. *On the first,* place the name of the stock and alongside the prices recorded at intervals. On the *third line* record the earnings for the past three years and the latest interim report. Obtain the average earnings for the past three years including the latest interim report. In the case of Ford, the 3-year earnings per share were $4.56 for 1954, $6.33 for 1955, and $5.63 for 1956. *On the second line* record the price-earning ratio. The introduction of another color such as red or blue for the p/e ratios will distinguish them. It might be advisable to use a distinctive color for the average earnings.

The average of the last three years for Ford was $5.51 per share. For General Motors it was $6.56 and for Chrysler it was $4.93 a share.

On 4/27/67 Ford closed at $54 ¼. At this price it was selling at approximately 10 times its 3-year earnings. General Motors at $84 ¾ was selling at 13 times its 3-year average and Chrysler at 43 ⅞ was 9.3 times. By recording the closing prices at regular intervals the changing p/e ratios can readily be seen.

How to determine the average earnings for the last three years

Inasmuch as our calculations are based on average earnings for the last three years we should learn how to determine the average not only for the annual reports but also for the interim ones. Assume earnings as follows:

	Year 1	$4.56	per share
	Year 2	6.33	per share
	Year 3	5.63	per share
First quarter	Year 4	1.10	per share
First half	Year 4	2.44	per share
9 months	Year 4	1.76	per share

Example 1. Average earnings for years 1, 2, and 3.

Add the 3 annual reports and divide by 3
The sum is $16.52.
1/3 of $16.52 is $5.51

Example 2. Three-year average to include *first quarter* of the
4th year.

Take 3/4 of year	1	$ 3.41
Add year	2	6.33
Add year	3	5.63
Add first quarter of year	4	1.10
Add the 4 figures to get		$16.47

1/3 of $16.47 is $5.49

Example 3. Three-year average to include first half-year report of 4th year.

Take 1/2 of year	1	$ 2.28
Add year	2	6.33
Add year	3	5.63
Add first half of year	4	2.44
Add the 4 figures to get		$16.68

1/3 of $16.68 is $5.56

Example 4. Three-year average to include first 9-month report.

Take 1/4 of year	1	$ 1.14
Add year	2	6.33
Add year	3	5.63
Add 9-month report		1.76
Add the 4 figures to get		$14.86

1/3 of $14.86 is $4.95

Exceptions

There are two exceptions that should be noted:

1. In the case of companies whose earnings are seasonal, do
not use the method described above. Instead, get the Standard
& Poor report, eliminate the comparable period three years ago
and replace it by current earnings. This applies especially to the
department and variety store group, most of whose earnings are
made in the last half of the year. The earnings for the first and
second quarter are usually negligible. Replace them by the

comparable earnings three years ago. This information is available at your brokers.

2. Utility earnings are usually quite steady. *The latest annual* report may be used instead of the 3-year average.

Summary of Chapter

There are many companies whose operations are sufficiently similar to be compared. Their securities constitute a homogenous group. If they meet all the other tests that will be described, including the Chapter 1 tests, the one with the lowest p/e ratio will usually be the best buy.

Division of Securities Listed on the New York Stock Exchange

The following is a listing of corporate securities, on the New York Stock Exchange, arranged by industries. It is not complete. However, it offers the investor a guide which he can use for comparison purposes. He can match others in which he is interested.

AIR CONDITIONING

Carrier
Trane Co.

AIR BRAKES

New York Air Brake
Westinghouse Air Brake

AIRCRAFT

Bendix Aviation
Boeing Co.
Douglas Aircraft
General Dynamics
North American Aviation

AIRCRAFT PRODUCTS

Ling Temco Vought
Utd. Aircraft

AIR LINES

American Airlines
Eastern Airlines
Northwest Airlines
United Airlines

ALUMINUM & ALUMINUM PROD.

Aluminum Co. of America
Alcan
Reynolds Metals

APPAREL MFRS.

Bobbie Brooks
Cluett Peabody
Munsingwear
Russ Togs

AUTOMOBILES

Chrysler Corp.
Ford
General Motors

AUTO SUPPLY

Borg Warner
Clark Equipment
Eaton Mfg.
Hayes Ind.
Kelsey Hayes
Rockwell Stand

BAKERY PRODUCTS
(BISCUITS)

National Biscuit
Keebler

BAKERY PRODUCTS (BREAD)

American Bakeries
Continental Baking
General Baking

BANKING EQUIPMENT

Diebold
Mosler Safe

BANKING (HOLDING CO.)

Marine Midland
Northwestern Bancorp.
Chase Manhattan Bank

BATTERIES

Eltra
ESB Corp.
Gould National

BEARING (ROLLER)

Clevite
Hoover Ball Bearing
Timken

BOWLING ALLEYS

Brunswick Corp.
American Machine & Foundry

BREWERIES

Associated Brew
Falstaff

BUILDING PLUMBERS SUP.

American Standard
Crane Co.

BUILDING ROOFING

Johns Manville
Ruberoid

BUILDING WALL PRODUCTS

Armstrong Cork
U. S. Gypsum

CAMERAS & PHOTO EQUIPMENT

Bell & Howell
Eastman Kodak
Polaroid
Xerox

CEMENT

Alpha Portland
General Portland
Missouri Portland Cement
Penn Dixie

CERAMICS

Ferro
Intl. Pipe & Ceramics

CHEMICALS (CHLORINE & CAUSTIC SODA)

Diamond Alkali
Hooker Chemical

CHEMICALS (COKE)

Koppers
Pittsburgh Coke

CHEMICALS (DETERGENTS)

Norton
Purex

CHEMICALS (DIVERSIFIED)

Allied
American Cyanamid
Dow
Du Pont
Monsanto
Olin Mathieson
Union Carbide

CHEMICALS (CELLULOSE)

Hercules Inc.
Rayonier
Celanese

CHEMICALS (GASES)

Air Products
Air Reduction
Chemetron

CHEMICALS (INORGANIC)

American Potash
Pennsalt
Stauffer
U. S. Borax

CHEMICALS (INK & CARBON)

Interchemical
Sun Chemical

CHEMICALS (ORGANIC)

Nalco
National Starch
Witco

CHEMICALS (PLASTIC PROD.)

Amerace
Reichhold
Thiokol
VSI

CHEMICALS (SULFUR)

Freeport
Texas Gulf Sulfur
Rohm & Haas

CLOCKS & WATCHES

Bulova Watch
General Time

CLOSED-END FUNDS

Abacus
Adams Express
American International
Dominick
Lehman Corp.
Madison Fund
Transamerica
Tri Continental

COAL (SOFT)

North American Coal
Peabody
Pittston

CONFECTIONERY

Tootsie Roll
Hershey
Wrigley W. Jr.

CONTAINERS (METAL & GLASS)

American Can
Continental Can

COPPER & NONFERROUS

American Metal Climax
American Smelting
Anaconda
Cerro
International Nickel
Kennecott Copper
Phelps Dodge
U. S. Smelting & Rfg.

COSMETICS

Avon Products
Colgate Palmolive
Revlon

CREDIT

CIT
Coml. Credit

SMALL LOAN COMPANIES

American Investment
Beneficial Finance
Budget Finance
General Acceptance
Household Finance

CREDIT SAVINGS & LOAN

Financial Federation
First Charter Finance
Gibraltar

DEPT. DISCOUNT & MAIL ORDER

Allied Stores
Assoc. Dry Goods
Federated Dept. Stores
Gimbel
Macy
Marshall Field

DRINKS (SOFT)

Canada Dry
Coca Cola
Pepsi Co.

DRUGS (ETHICAL)

Abbott Lab.
American Home Prod.
Merck
Pfizer
Schering
Smith Kline & French
Upjohn

DRUGSTORES

Cunningham
Peoples Drug
Walgreen

DRUGS (PROPRIETARY)

Bristol Myers
McKesson & Robbins
Norwich
Plough
Warner Lambert

ELECT. DIVERSIFIED

General Electric.
Westinghouse

ELECT. CONTROLS

Cutler Hammer
Foxboro
Square D

ELECTRONICS

AMP Inc.
Avco
Beckman Inst.
Collins Radio
Emerson Elect.
General Instrument
General Precision
Honeywell
Ling Temco
Texas Instrument

ENGINES (COMPRESSORS)

American Bosch
Briggs & Stratton

FLOOR COVERINGS

Congoleum Nairn
Mohasco Ind.

FOOD (DAIRY)

Foremost
National Dairy

FOOD (DIVERSIFIED)

Allied Mills
Beatrice
Beechnut Life Savers
Borden
Campbell Soup
General Foods
Std. Brands

FOOD (FLOUR & CEREALS)

Corn Products
General Mills
Quaker Oats

FOOD (MEAT PROD.)

Armour
Swift

FREIGHTAGE

Interstate Motor Freight
McLean
Ryder System
U. S. Freight

FURNITURE MFG.

American Seating
Drexel Enterprises

GLASS (TECHNICAL)

Corning
Owens Illinois

GLASS (WINDOW FLAT)

Libbey-Owens-Ford
Pittsburgh Plate

GLASS CONTAINERS

Anchor Hocking

GROCERIES

Allied Supermarkets
Acme
Great A & P
Kroger
Safeway

HOUSEHOLD APPLIANCES

Maytag
McGraw Edison
Sunbeam
Whirlpool

LAUNDRY LINENS

Consol Laundries
National Service

INSURANCE

Continental Ins.
Ins. Co. of North America

LAND LEASING

Great Northern Iron Ore
Kern County Land

LIQUOR

American Distilling Co.
Distillers Corp.—Seagrams Ltd.
National Distillers & Chem.

MACHINERY (BOILERS)

Babcock & Wilcox
Combustion Engineering

MACHINERY (BELTING)

Rex Chainbelt
Link Belt

MACHINERY (EXCAVATION)

Bucyrus Erie
Caterpillar Tractor
Gardner Denver
Ingersoll Rand

MACHINERY (FARM)

Allis Chalmers
Case J. I.
Deere & Co.
International Harvester

MACHINERY (HEAVY)

Blaw Knox
Bliss E. W.
Stone & Webster

MACHINERY (PRINTING)

Harris Intertype
Eltra

MACHINERY (TOOLS)

Black & Decker
Chicago Pneumatic Tool
Cincinnati Milling
National Acme

MOTION PICTURE PROD.

Columbia Pictures
Loews Theatres
MGM

OFFICE EQUIPMENT

Addressograph-Multigraph
Burroughs
International Business Mach.
National Cash Register

OILS (DOMESTIC)

Ashland
Atlantic Richfield
Cities Service
Phillips Petroleum
Sinclair
Std. Oil Ohio
Union Oil California

OIL INTERNATIONAL

Gulf
Royal Dutch
Mobil Oil
Std. Oil California
Std. Oil New Jersey
Texaco Inc.

OIL EQUIPMENT

Dover Corp.
Dresser Industries
McDermott

PAINTS

Glidden
National Lead
Sherwin Williams Co.

PAPER (WHITE & BOOK)

Hammermill
Kimberly Clark
Mead Corp.
West Virginia Pulp

PAPER (NEWSPRINT)

Crown Zellerbach
Great Northern Paper

PAPER (BOXBOARD & KRAFT)

Chesapeake Corp. Va.
International Paper
Union Bag Camp

PRINTING & PUBLISHING

Crowell Collier
Ginn & Co.
Harcourt, Brace & World
McGraw Hill
National Periodical
Grolier

RADIO & TV BROADCASTING

American Broadcasting
Columbia Broadcasting
Metromedia
Storer
Taft

RAILROADS (CENTRAL WESTERN)

Chicago, Milwaukee
Denver & Rio Grande

RAILROADS (CENTRAL EASTERN)

Norfolk & Western
Pennsylvania

RAILROADS (SOUTHERN)

Atlantic Coast Line
Gulf, Mobile & Ohio
Louisville & Nashville

RAILROADS (SOUTH WESTERN)

Atchison, Topeka & Santa Fe
Kansas City Southern
Southern Pacific
Missouri Pacific "A"

RAILROAD EQUIPMENT

Amsted Ind.
General Signal
General Steel Ind.
Poor & Co.

RAILROAD PARTS (CARS)

ACF Industries
Pullman
Union Tank Car

RAZOR MFRS.

Gillette Co.
Eversharp

REAL ESTATE & HOTELS

Hilton Hotels
Sheraton Hotels

RESTAURANTS

Howard Johnson
Stouffer Foods
Shattuck F.G.

RETAIL STORES (SPECIALTY)

American News
Book of The Month
Gamble Skogmo

RETAIL STORES (VARIETY CHAINS)

Grant W.T.
Kresge S.S.
McCrory
Woolworth

RETAIL VENDING

ABC Consolidated
Servomation

RUBBER (TIRES)

Firestone Tire & Rubber
Goodrich B.F. Co.
Goodyear Tire & Rubber
Uniroyal

SCREWS, NUTS, BOLTS

Elastic Stop Nut
Std. Pressed Steel
Utd. Carr Fastener

SHIPBUILDING & REPAIRING

American Shipbuilding
Merritt Chapman & Scott
N.Y. Shipbuilding

STEAMSHIP LINES

Barber Oil
Moore & McCormack
U.S. Lines

SHOES

Brown Shoe
Endicott Johnson
Melville Shoe Corp.

SOAP

Colgate Palmolive
Procter & Gamble

STEEL

Armco Steel
Bethlehem Steel
National Steel
Republic Steel
U.S. Steel

STEEL ACCESSORIES

General Refractories
Harbison Walker
Mesta Machine

SUGAR

Amalgamated
Great Western Sugar
American Sugar Ref.

SURGICAL DRESSINGS

American Hospital Supply
Becton, Dickinson
Johnson & Johnson
Kendall

TEXTILES (COTTON)

Burlington Ind.
Stevens J.P.
Utd. Merchants & Mfg.
West Point Pepperell

TOBACCO (CIGARETTES)

American Tobacco
Liggett & Myers
Lorillard
Phillip Morris

TOBACCO (CIGARS)

Bayuk
Consol Cigar
General Cigar

TRANSPORTATION (AUTO. BUSES)

Greyhound
Hertz

VENDING MACHINES

Canteen Corp.
Vendo

VEGETABLE & ANIMAL OILS

Anderson Clayton
Archer Daniels
Central Soya

WATER WORKS

American Water Works
Hackensack Water

WOOD PRODUCTS & LUMBER

Diamond International
Georgia Pacific
Weyerhaeuser

WRITING INSTRUMENTS

Eversharp
Parker Pen

WIRE & CABLE

American Chain & Cable
General Cable
Essex Wire

5
Security Analysis

The starting point for sound investing is to determine the stability of the structure, the growth pattern, and the ability of a company to maintain its position among its competitors. This is the essence of the tests that should be applied. It should also be applied to companies in an industry, because not all are equally sound. In the auto industry, for example, American Motors cannot be classed with Chrysler, Ford or General Motors. This does not mean that it should not be bought. At some point it may interest speculators or traders.

There is a procedure that this chapter will suggest for those who wish to invest in a specific security or group. If the interest is in a specific security it should be analyzed along with the group whose operations are comparable.

The statistical information that is needed is contained in a Standard & Poor report and the annual and interim statements issued by the company. The address of a company is included in the Standard & Poor report.

A group analysis consists of two parts: a balance sheet and profit and loss statement. The first describes the structure of the company; the second the factors that result in profits or losses.

The method will be explained by studying the air conditioning group, which is typical of others.

There are three important securities in this field:

Carrier Corporation
Fedders Corporation
Trane Company

Qualifying Tests

The analysis begins with a series of five qualifying tests. These are limited to comparing specific balance sheet and profit and loss items to discover those securities that are marginal. These preliminary tests are not intended to select the best value.

The first set of three tests will be confined to the balance sheets. Here are the balance sheets of the three companies condensed from their annual reports.

**Balance Sheet
Carrier Corp.
as of October 31, 1966**

ASSETS
Current Assets

Cash and Marketable Securities	$ 52,604,168
Receivables	60,342,371
Total Inventories	100,913,041
Total Current Assets	$213,859,580
Investments, Prepaid Expenses, etc.	13,735,911
Property, Plant and Equipment	73,681,744
Total Assets	$301,277,235

LIABILITIES AND STOCKHOLDERS' EQUITY

Total Current Liabilities	$ 75,200,242
Long-Term Debt	42,787,000
Stockholders' Equity	
Cumulative Preferred Stock	9,075,600*
Common Stockholders' Equity	174,214,393
Total Liabilities and Stockholders' Equity	$301,277,235

Summary of the Balance Sheet of Carrier Corporation

Total Assets	$301 million
Total Liabilities	127 million*
Common Stockholders' Equity	174 million*

* Note that $9 million of the preferred stock was added to the liabilities and substracted from the stockholder's equity. This analysis is being made from the point of view of the common stockholder and the preferred stock of $9 million represents a prior claim. Technically, a preferred stockholder is not a liability.

Assets equal Liabilities plus Common Stockholders' Equity

$301 million   = $127 million   + $174 million

Balance Sheet
Fedders Corporation
as of August 31, 1966

ASSETS

Current Assets

Cash	$ 4,108,000
Accounts Receivable	20,349,000
Inventories	11,725,000
Total Current Assets	$36,182,000
Other Assets	5,055,000
Property, Plant and Equipment, at Cost:	16,377,000
Total Assets	$57,614,000

LIABILITIES AND STOCKHOLDERS' EQUITY

Total Current Liabilities	$ 9,548,000
Long-Term Debt	19,621,000
Common Stockholders' Equity	28,445,000
Total Liabilities and Stockholders' Equity	$57,614,000

Summary of Balance Sheet of Fedders Corporation (numbers rounded)

Total Assets	$57.6 million
Total Liabilities	29.2 million
Common Stockholders' Equity	28.4 million

Assets equal Liabilities plus Common Stockholders' Equity.

$57.6 million   = $29.2 million   + $28.4 million

Balance Sheet
The Trane Company
December 31, 1967

ASSETS

Cash	$ 10,640,076
Receivables	43,052,895
Inventories & Sundries	45,769,187
Total Current Assets	$ 99,462,158
Property, Plant and Equipment	44,150,748
Total Assets	$143,612,906

LIABILITIES AND STOCKHOLDERS' EQUITY

Total Current Liabilities	$ 24,382,839
Long-Term Debt	26,965,080
Common Stockholders' Equity	92,264,987
Total Liabilities and Stockholders' Equity	$143,612,906

Summary of Balance Sheet of The Trane Company (figures rounded)

Total Assets	$143.6 million
Total Liabilities	51.3 million
Stockholders' Equity	92.3 million

Assets equal Liabilities plus Common Stockholders' Equity.

$143.6 million   = $51.3 million   + $92.3 million

Using the information in the balance sheets we are now equipped to make three important qualifying tests.

Test No. 1
Liquidity or Working Capital

The first qualifying test is: How liquid is the company? Does it have sufficient assets to meet current liabilities? This information can be obtained from the balance sheet of the company and the lower half of the Standard & Poor's report.

A company has to be able to meet its current obligations. It must meet its payroll, taxes, utility bills, notes to banks, interest payments to banks and bondholders, etc. These are called *current liabilities*. They are debts that will fall due within the year.

The funds to meet current liabilities will come from cash on hand, money due from customers, merchandise inventory, etc. These are called *current assets*. The difference between current assets and current liabilities is called *working capital*.

Here is an analysis of the current assets, current liabilities, working capital, and the ratio of current assets to current liabilities.

Current Assets – Current Liabilities = Working Capital

Company	(1)	–	(2)	=	(3)

	Current Assets	Current Liabilities	Working Capital	Ratio (1) : (2)
Carrier	$214 million	$75 million	$139 million	2.9 to 1
Fedders	36 million	10 million	26 million	3.6 to 1
Trane	99 million	24 million	75 million	4.1 to 1

Looking at the extreme right, this chart indicates that Carrier had $2.90 (2.9 to 1), Fedders $3.60 (3.6 to 1) and Trane $4.10 (4.1 to 1) for *every dollar* of current liabilities. This is satisfactory. One should not conclude that the greater the working capital the better the company. A well-managed company needs only enough working capital to meet its obligations. It is not a bank. It does not need an excess. As a matter of fact, if its working capital is too great, further investigation should be made. For example, one of the items in current assets is inventory; that is, merchandise made for sale, but not sold when the report was prepared. If the company has too much inventory, that may be bad if sales lag. It may result in losses.

How is what is satisfactory determined? The general rule is: *Let the group decide.* In the air conditioning field a ratio of from 3 or 4 to 1 appears to be normal. In the oils and utilities it is much lower. These are businesses where turnover is rapid and there is no need for large working capital.

Where a company's liquidity is significantly below its group, it is safest to stay away. There have been companies that were forced into receivership or bankruptcy because they couldn't meet their current liabilities. The liquidity test spots these quickly.

There is still another test within the framework of liquidity that is recommended. It is *cash* to current liability. Is the cash position satisfactory? Current assets include inventory, which may be top-heavy. The management may have miscalculated. The working capital test may appear satisfactory. However, if it is short of cash and long on inventory there may be trouble ahead. The cash to current liability test serves still another worthy function. It exposes the "cats" and "dogs" that sell "over the counter." There are numerous securities of the "penny" variety whose cash position is so bad they could become bankrupt momentarily. There is no point speculating in these. They represent total risk.

The *liquidity test* should be used only to expose the weak-structured companies. It should not be used to buy securities. The p/e ratio and Chapter 1 spread tests should serve that purpose.

Test No. 2
Total Liabilities to Total Assets

A company cannot operate comfortably if its working capital is inadequate. However, it may be adequate, and yet the company may be weak structurally. This will be uncovered by comparing total liablities and total assets. This is the second qualifying test.

Turn to the three balance sheets.

Company	(1) Total Liabilities	(2) Total Assets	(3) Ratio (1) to (2)
Carrier	$127 million	$301 million	.42
Fedders	29 million	58 million	.51
Trane	51 million	144 million	.37

Column (3) indicates that for every dollar of assets in the Carrier Company $.42 belongs to the creditors, including those who hold preferred stock, and $.58 belongs to the common stockholders. In the case of Fedders, for every dollar of assets $.51 belongs to the creditors and $.49 to the common stockholders. For Trane, $.37 belongs to the creditors and $.67 to the common stockholders.

All the assets of a business do not belong to the common stockholders. The assets represent all the financial items over which the company has legal control. It includes cash in banks, merchandise, buildings, land, furniture, fixtures, raw materials, goods in work, inventory, accounts receivable (this means money due from customers), etc. Against the assets the company owes debts to creditors for merchandise, to workers, utilities, government for taxes, banks for loans, etc. Subtract the liabilities from the assets and obtain the common stockholders' equity. This is the *part* of the assets that belongs to the common stockholders. In short, the common stockholders own only part of the assets.

Here is a simplified structure picture of the three companies:

	Assets	=	Liabilities	+	Common Stockholders' Equity
Carrier	$301 million	=	$127 million	+	$174 million
Fedders	57.6 million	=	29.2 million	+	28.4 million
Trane	143.6 million	=	51.3 million	+	92.3 million

Reducing these figures for each dollar of assets, the structure picture looks like this:

	Assets	=	Liabilities	+	Common Stockholders' Equity
Carrier	$1	=	$.42	+	$.58
Fedders	1	=	.51	+	.49
Trane	1	=	.37	+	.63

What Is Good?

When is the structure sturdy? In general, let the group decide. What may be good for the utilities may not be for the oils. Each operates in a manner which meets its personal needs. In air conditioning Carrier and Trane are, in our opinion, better structured because their liabilities are less than their stockholders' equity. Where the liabilities are too large for the total assets there may be trouble during adverse times. Large debts result in large interest charges. When business is good, these can be met easily. In fact, they usually boost income because interest charges are small by comparison to profits. However, when conditions become bad they represent a burden. The term "leverage" is normally used to indicate the ratio of debt structure to total assets. High leverage would mean a large debt structure and small leverage a small one. Where the leverage is high exercise additional care.

Test No. 3
Common Stockholders' Equity Growth

The third qualifying test is this: Does the company set aside enough funds from its annual profits to insure its growth so that it can keep abreast of the industry? Or does it distribute all its profits to its stockholders and put little or nothing aside for future expansion?

Growth can be measured by the expansion of the common stockholders' equity. In a corporation these are transformed into *book value*. If you divide the common stockholders' equity by the number of shares of stock that are outstanding you get book value. In short, *book value* is the common stockholders' equity of 1 share of stock.

Here is the book value of the three air conditioning stocks:

Security	Common Stockholders' Equity from Annual Report	Number of Shares of Common Stock Outstanding	Book Value
Carrier	$174 million	7,510,000	$23.25
Fedders	28.4 million	2,141,648	13.20
Trane	92.2 million	5,388,004	17.10

Undistributed profits increase the book value and losses decrease it. Corporations normally distribute part of their profits to their stockholders as dividends and reinvest the remainder for expansion. It is the reinvested portion of the profits that determines the increase in the book value.

Examine the increase in the book value of the three during the last decade:

Increase in Book Value of 3 Air Conditioning Companies

Company	Latest Book Value	Book Value Ten Years Ago	Percent Increase
Carrier	$23.25	$16.35	44
Fedders	13.20	9.49	39
Trane	17.12	7.59	126

This information can be obtained from Standard & Poor's reports.

The capital growth of the three companies appears to be satisfactory. Trane has reinvested more of its profits than the other two. This isolated fact may not be too significant.

One should be concerned where the book value of a company does not keep pace with its competitors, or even falls behind. For example, the book value of Endicott Johnson fell from $71.84 per share in 1957 to $56.00 at the end of 1966. This was caused by a sharp drop in profits during the period. (Management appears to have reversed the trend.)

The growth in book value is normally associated with increased operations. Sales increase; so do profits. It can be likened to getting more interest from increased deposits in a savings account. However, one should not assume that the relationship is mechanical. There are times when book value increases and profits decline. These are exceptions. For most companies, and over a period of years, they keep pace with each other.

The liquidity or working capital test, the total liability test, and the book value test serve only to spot the marginal companies. They should not be used to select the best comparative value. There are three additional tests. These are taken from the Profit and Loss Statement.

Test No. 4
Sales Growth

The fourth qualifying test is sales growth. Has the company maintained its position in its industry? Has it moved ahead or

Sales Growth of 3 Air Conditioning Stocks

Company	Sales Latest Annual Report	Sales Ten Years Ago	Percent Increase
Carrier	$400 million	$263	50
Fedders	62 million	71	(11) decrease
Trane	188 million	81	130

fallen behind? The answer lies in an examination of the three. The information was obtained from Standard & Poor's and company reports (see bottom of facing page).

It is quite evident that Fedders has fallen behind its competitors. This automatically eliminates it for investors who seek a sound, growth company. However, it may be considered by those who are speculatively minded, who may want to purchase it when it conforms to the Chapter 1 tests. There are individuals who do quite well buying and selling marginal companies by careful timing (see Chapter 2).

Test No. 5
Profits Growth

The fifth and last qualifying test is profits growth. Has the company's profits kept pace with its competitors? This is the acid test of management and efficiency. Let us put the three to this test:

Profit Growth of 3 Air Conditioning Companies
(Adjusted for splits and stock dividends)

Company	Profits Per Share Latest Annual Report	Profits Per Share Ten Years Ago	Increase in Profits
Carrier	$2.83	$1.06	170%
Fedders	.55	2.57	(80%) decrease
Trane	2.46	1.17	110%

(Information from Standard & Poor's reports)

This analysis confirms the observation made under Sales Growth that Fedders is not in the class of the other two. It must be ranked as a speculation; the others as investment grade. Such a company should be considered only by those who realize the risk they are taking and who want to take advantage of normal market fluctuations.

It can be understood from the analysis why Carrier which

sold at a much lower p/e ratio than Trane during the last decade has been moving upward slowly and steadily. It has done well.

Summary of the Qualifying Tests

The five tests have served only one purpose: *to separate the better-quality securities from the poorer ones.* They should not be used as the basis for buying a security. They should not be viewed mechanically. Sales growth, for example, might be the result of acquisition, good or bad. Profits obtained by comparing current earnings vs. those ten years ago might obscure the fact that one or the other may have been an abnormal year and not representative.

Another factor that should be considered is the trend of the industry. Ten years ago it may have been excellent, followed by a slump. It may now be in a recovery period. However, the earnings may still be behind what they were a decade ago. For example, the oil security earnings suffered quite a slump but recovered significantly during the past few years. Judgment rather than mechanical number reading should govern decision making. The numbers are only guides. Judgment is decisive.

Test No. 6
The P/E Ratio

The decisive test is the p/e ratio. This determines how much one is paying for each dollar of earnings. This ratio should be determined the day that the stock is considered for *actual purchase.* All the previous tests are *background information* and should be done in advance.

Here are the p/e ratios of the three:

Price-Earning Ratios of 3 Air Conditioning Companies

Company	Closing Price of Stock July 10, 1967	Average Earnings Last Three Annual Reports*	P/E Ratio
Carrier	$67	$2.28	29x
Fedders	26	1.20	22x
Trane	59	2.21	27x

*Not adjusted for interim reports.

The lowest p/e ratio stock is Fedders. Because of its poor sales and profit growth performance it is not recommended despite its excellent market performance during 1967. The average investor, who can devote a small amount of his time to this activity, would do better to confine himself to quality companies.

What about Carrier and Trane? These should not be considered because both p/e ratios are too high, Trane much too high. This does not mean that they will not do well in the future. They may, but the risk on the downside is large for a security selling above 20x earnings. Herein is contained a philosophy of investment. There are those who buy good-quality securities at any price. From what has been stated previously, and will be repeated in different ways in the future, this reasoning is not judged as valuable as limiting commitments to lower p/e ratios where the yields are larger.

The p/e ratio test, though quite important, should not be the final arbiter. The Chapter 1 spread tests should be made before a purchase. Those who follow p/e ratios only will suffer losses on a sufficient number of low p/e ratios stocks of good quality, bought at the wrong time. There are many people who complain that they own only "blue chips" which have done miserably. Chapter 1 tests will tell them why. They are a safety valve, and should not be neglected.

There are two more calculations that should be made:

Calculation No. 1—Yield

How much does one earn who invests in the three securities? Here is a table from which this information can be obtained:

Yield on 3 Air Conditioning Securities

Company	Closing Price of Stock May 29, 1967	Dividend	Yield
Carrier	$67	$1.00	1.5%
Fedders	26	.60	2.2
Trane	59	.80	1.4

The yield here is much too low on both Carrier and Trane to be considered for investment for the average person.

Calculation No. 2—Cash-Flow

There is a final calculation that every investor and trader should be aware of. It is the cash-flow.

Cash-flow is the amount of money that remains with the company after paying all expenses, including taxes. *It is the sum of profits and depreciation charges.* The balance after paying dividends and installments on a debt can be used for corporate expansion.

Here are the cash-flow figures for the three air conditioning stocks:

Cash-Flow for 3 Air Conditioning Securities for 1966

Company	Total Profits after Taxes	Depreciation	Cash-Flow
Carrier	$21,600,000	$7,280,000	$28,880,000
Fedders	1,100,000	900,000	2,000,000
Trane	13,280,000	5,610,000	18,890,000

In the case of Carrier, the company's cash-flow was almost $29 million, for Fedders $2 million, and for Trane almost $19 million. In some companies the depreciation charges are small, in others, especially the oil, steel, movies, and airline groups, they are quite large. In some steel companies the depreciation charges are larger than earnings. In 1966, for example, Youngstown Sheet and Tube declared earnings after taxes of $42.8 million. Provision for depreciation and depletion amounted to $48.5 million. This gave the company a cash-flow of $91 million. After paying dividends of $19 million and repaying $5.7 million on its long-term debt it retained $65 million which it was using for its modernization program.

Why do depreciation and depletion charges affect the cash-flow?

The income tax laws permit a company to charge *as an expense* that part of its wasting assets that will become valueless in time. If a building is expected to become worthless in 25 years, the company may charge 1/25 of its cost as an expense annually in computing its income tax. In the case of minerals the company may charge as an expense the value of the deterioration of its land because of their depletion. The oil companies are allowed to deduct as an expense 27½% of the value of the oil that is taken from its wells. This "percentage depletion," as it is called, is permitted as long as the well produces oil, without regard to the original cost of the drilling.

The companies that have large depreciation charges and hence significant cash-flows can use the sums for expansion purposes. When studying the earnings of a company the cash-flow should be noticed. Sometimes earnings are masked by large depreciation charges. For example, for 1966 the earnings for American Airlines were $52 million or $5.80 per share. The depreciation charges were $66 million or $7.10 per share.

Summary of Analysis of 3 Air Conditioning Stocks

The information contained in the 5 qualifying tests, the 6th acid test and the 2 calculations may be summarized in the group comparison chart on pages 98 and 99.

Summary of Chapter

Chapter 5 presents a method for analyzing small or large groups, rather than individual securities. There are several qualifying tests to separate the better from the poorer-quality securities. The acid test is the p/e ratio of the better-quality issues. Once the quality has been determined the investor should refer to the Chapter 2 tests for timing. Buying a good-quality security at the wrong time may be less rewarding than buying one of poorer quality at the right time.

Industry   Air Conditioning

Security	Liquidity			Prior Obligations			Capital Growth		
	1 Curr. Asst. Millions	2 Curr. Liab. Millions	1 : 2	3 Prior Oblig. Millions	4 Total Assets Millions	3 : 4	5 Book Value 1966 Per Share	6 Book Value 1957 Per Share	5 : 6 % Incr.
Carrier	$214	$63	$3.4	$127	$301	.42	$23.25	$16.35	43
Fedders	37	9	4.1	29	58	.51	13.20	9.49	39
Trane	99	24	4.1	51	144	.37	17.10	7.59	126

Sales Growth			Profit Growth			Price Earning Ratio			Yield			Cash Flow Ratio		
7	8	7 : 8	9	10	9 : 10	11	12	11 : 12	13	14	13 : 14	15	16	15 : 16
1966 Sales Millions	1957 Sales Millions	% Incr.	1966 Profit Per Share	1957 Profit Per Share	% Incr.	Price of Stock Per Share	Av. Profit Per Share		Dividend Per Share	Price of Stock Per Share	%	Price of Stock	Cash Flow	
$400	$263	50	2.83	1.06	170	$67	$2.28	29X	$1.00	$67	1.8	$67	3.25	20.5
62	71	11 dec.	.55	2.57	80 dec.	26	1.20	22X	.60	26	3.2	26	1.62	16
188	81	130	2.46	1.17	110	59	2.21	27X	.80	59	1.4	59	3.25	18.2

HARDY & CO.

MEMBERS

· NEW YORK STOCK EXCHANGE
· AMERICAN STOCK EXCHANGE
25 BROAD STREET · NEW YORK 4

Digby 4-7800

6
Areas of Investment

Holding on to money is no easy matter. Those who have it are surrounded by temptations. The most sinister is within the person: his greed or need to speculate. It entices him to take chances to make more—which too often he does not really need. It misdirects him into bizarre channels to avoid paying income taxes. It pushes him from one error to another. Perhaps the logical way to start an investment program is by a critical self-analysis.

The first thing to learn about having money is that risk cannot be avoided. Whether it is kept in a mattress, placed in an insured savings bank, invested in government bonds, prime securities, real estate, land, jewelry, gold, silver, antiques, etc., there is always a risk. There are different kinds of risks, but they are all there.

What about money in banks?

Money in insured savings institutions is safe. It is readily available and can be obtained simply by writing your name on a withdrawal slip. The funds on deposit are insured by agencies of the government.

But there is a risk and a great one at that. It is inflation: the deterioration of buying power. For the past few decades there has been a slow, steady erosion of the buying power of money. The pace was accelerated in 1967 because of the demands of

101

the Vietnam war. Here is a table showing the declining buying power since 1930. The figures were adapted from government statistics on the cost of living index.

Cost of $1 Worth of Consumers' Goods in 1930

Year	Cost of Consumers' Goods
1930	$1.00
1940	.82
1950	1.40
1960	1.72
Dec. 1965	1.85
Dec. 1966	1.91
Dec. 1967	2.00

What does it avail one to receive 5% interest from his bank, pay income taxes on it and end with a loss of buying power? To keep all one's money in insured savings institutions involves a very great risk.

There are a few banks which are not insured. They offer their depositors a larger rate of interest than do the insured banks. We advise people to shun them. The risk involved far outweighs the small additional reward.

How about gilt-edge bonds and other fixed-income securities?

There are many bonds of high quality, including U.S. Governments, tax-exempts, and corporate issues. The interest can be depended on to be paid regularly to maturity. The principal is secure. But the risk involved is the same as it is for deposits in insured banks. The deterioration of the buying power of the dollar affects *all fixed-income investments—no exceptions.*

How about other areas of investment?

Real estate, securities, and other areas of investment involve risk of one kind or another. They require judgment, study, caution, and constant attention. Nothing is static. Change is eternal. The investor must be vigilant, especially avoiding investments that appeal to his greed or aversion to paying income taxes. We stress the latter because it is so universal and too often leads people to trouble.

With this brief introduction, consider the major areas of investment that are available.

Banks

There are three types of banks where individuals can deposit their money.

Savings Banks

Saving and Loan Associations

Commercial Banks

These are insured by the Federal Deposit Insurance Company or the Savings and Loan Insurance Company, both agencies of the United States Government. The amount one should have in savings banks depends on the economic status of the individual. If one has a good position, is professional, is saving regularly, and has reason to believe that this condition should continue for the foreseeable future, he should keep approximately *one year's expenditure in the bank*. Thus, if he normally spends $15,000 annually he should always have that amount readily available for contingencies. The remainder of his cash should be invested in equities. If he is retired or his earnings are not sufficient for normal needs so that he depends on additional income from interest or dividends, he should keep *at least two year's* expenditures in the bank. The rest should be invested in equities.

Private Loans

There are individuals who discover merchants who have great need to continuously borrow substantial sums of money and who are willing to pay large rates of interest as high as 15 or even 20%. Such tempting offers touch the vital greed areas of normal people. They start with small investments, increasing as interest payments are regularly received. They spread the "good" news to friends who join them. All goes well until the day of disaster.

It should not be assumed that the borrowers are all dishonest. To be sure, there are swindlers among them. However, many of them are merchants in financial difficulty who cannot borrow from banks at normal rates of interest. They must pay exorbitant rates to remain in business. The risk is great and the failures many.

Widows and retired individuals are easy victims. They need more income than can be obtained from normal channels. Friends and relatives often excite them with lurid tales, naming "smart" people who are involved. The temptation is too difficult to resist.

Don't get started. It's like taking dope. Once begun it is difficult to stop.

Bonds
Bonds are evidences of obligations to pay. They are more formal instruments than promissory notes. There are several essential features to a bond.

1. Rate of interest. This is fixed and payable at definite dates. Most bonds have interest coupons attached to them, each bearing the amount due and the dates payable. The investor cuts the coupon and deposits it in his bank as he would a check. The purchaser's name does not appear on the face of the bond. There are a few bonds which are registered in the name of the investor. Interest is paid directly by the company to the registered owner.

2. Maturity. A bond has a maturity date. It may be a few months hence or a long time off. When the date of maturity arrives the bond must be paid in full, regardless of the buyer's cost. The date of maturity is an integral part of the bond.

3. Callability. There are bonds that may be called at a specified price by the issuing corporation prior to their maturity. This provision must be stated clearly on the bond when it is issued. Those who buy bonds should be aware of this feature. This is especially important in a rising bond market or for convertible bonds. Buying a convertible bond above its call value involves a risk because the company may decide to redeem it. For example, Collins Radio has a convertible bond which may be redeemed by the company at 102¾. This means at $1,027.50 for each $1,000 bond. In 1957 the bonds were selling as high as $1,540 per bond, for reasons that will be explained when we consider convertible bonds. The investor in these bonds should be aware of this fact. This does not mean that he should not buy them. There are other considerations which may make them attractive.

When a bond is purchased in the open market the buyer pays the price agreed upon, plus interest from the last interest date to the date of purchase. When he sells the bond he gets interest to the date of sale. When a bond has a blemish because interest is either not certain or has not been paid, it sells flat. Newspapers usually place the letter (F) next to such a bond when quoting its price.

We shall now consider the different kinds of bonds which can be purchased.

U.S. Government Bonds

The United States Government has many kinds of bonds, some with attractive features. There are the "E" bonds which are purchased at a discount and redeemed at face value when they mature. They are issued in the name of the investor and cannot be transferred to another person. No interest is paid until the bonds mature or are redeemed prior to that date. This interest is exempt from city and state income taxes but not from the Federal income tax.

For those who want short-term investments for one year or

less, there are *U.S. Treasury Bills.* They can be purchased directly from the Federal Reserve Bank each week (without fee) or on the open market. They are sold at a discount and redeemed at par. They can be bought and sold through banks or brokers. The interest is exempt from state and city taxes, but not from the Federal income tax. They are suitable for large institutions which have substantial sums they have to invest for short periods of time. Here is a list of Treasury Bill quotations of December 7, 1967.

Dec. 7, 1967

U.S. Treas. Bills

Mat	Bid	Ask	Mat	Bid	Ask
	Discount			Discount	
12-14	4.15	3.65	4- 4	5.10	4.95
12-21	4.10	3.60	4-11	5.19	5.00
12-28	4.10	3.60	4-18	5.20	5.05
12-31	4.50	3.85	4-22	5.21	5.15
1- 4	4.20	3.95	4-25	5.26	5.10
1-11	4.33	4.15	4-30	5.28	5.15
1-18	4.43	4.23	5- 2	5.34	5.20
1-25	4.45	4.29	5- 9	5.42	5.26
1-31	4.50	4.30	5-16	5.44	5.30
2- 1	4.65	4.56	5-23	5.46	5.36
2- 8	4.74	4.70	5-31	5.50	5.40
2-15	4.78	4.78	6- 6	5.50	5.44
2-23	4.84	4.78	6-24	5.51	5.47
2-29	4.86	4.80	6-30	5.52	5.40
3- 7	4.90	4.87	7-31	5.55	5.43
3-14	4.95	4.85	8-31	5.61	5.57
3-21	4.98	4.86	9-30	5.53	5.44
3-22	4.91	4.86	10-31	5.53	5.43
3-28	4.97	4.87	11-30	5.62	5.59
3-31	5.00	4.86		... ...	

Note the following:

1. Maturities are weekly, from December 14, 1967 to November 30, 1968.

2. They are traded on the open market on a bid and ask basis, the same as common stock. The 12-14 (1967) maturities, for example, were quoted as 4.15 bid and 3.65 ask. This means that the buyers of the bonds wanted to receive 4.15% to maturity and the sellers were willing to sell at a price that would yield only 3.65%. The spread between the bid and ask narrows as the maturity lengthens so that at the last one, 11-30 (1968), it is 5.62% bid and 5.59% ask. There are times when yields suddenly jump to more than 5% for Bills. At this yield they become especially attractive for individuals because the income is tax

exempt from city and state taxes. The commission is so small that some brokers will not accept orders for less than 10 bonds ($10,000) unless the buyer is willing to pay a larger fee.

For those who want to buy government bonds that mature within five years there are *Treasury Notes.* They can be bought and sold on the open market like other securities. Unlike the Bills they are not sold at a discount, but at the market price and redeemed at par ($1,000) when they mature. They should be watched for those periods, such as December 1967, when they were sold at prices to yield better than 5%. Here is a list of U.S. Treasury Notes from December 7, 1967:

Dec. 7, 1967

U.S. Treas. Notes

Rate	Mat	Bid	Asked	Yld
5⅝	2-68	100.3	100.5	4.70
1½	4-68	98.22	98.28	5.12
4¾	5-68	99.20	99.22	5.47
4¼	8-68	99.0	99.2	5.66
1½	10-68	97.2	97.6	5.06
5¼	11-68	99.20	99.22	5.60
5⅝	2-69	99.29	99.31	5.65
1½	4-69	95.10	95.18	5.03
1½	10-69	93.20	93.28	5.07
1½	4-70	92.0	92.4	5.15
1½	10-70	90.14	90.28	5.02
5	11-70	98.4	98.8	5.66
5⅜	2-71	99.4	99.8	5.64
1½	4-71	88.26	89.4	5.11
5¼	5-71	98.30	99.2	5.55
1½	10-71	87.6	87.22	5.09
5⅜	11-71	99.6	99.10	5.57
4¾	2-72	96.14	96.18	5.68
1½	4-72	85.16	86.16	5.02
4¾	5-72	96.4	96.8	5.72
1½	10-72	84.10	85.10	4.97
5¾	11-74	99.30	100.2	5.7[illegible]

It should be noted that the bid and ask quotations are given in 32nds of a dollar. The last Treasury Note quoted to mature in November 1974 is 99.30 bid 100.2 asked. This means $999.375 bid and $1,000.625 asked for a $1,000 note. The yield of this bond to maturity is 5.72%.

There are certain U.S. Government bonds that may be used to pay the Federal estate tax, in lieu of cash. They are accepted at par ($1,000 per bond) regardless of cost. Individuals who are well on in years and who wish to reduce the impact of the estate tax on their heirs might consider purchasing these bonds.

It should be noted that they must be in a person's portfolio when he passes away to obtain the tax benefit. The list is furnished by the Federal Reserve Bank. Here is a partial list of U.S. Government Bonds, which includes a few eligible for estate tax savings purposes.

Government, Agency and Miscellaneous Securities

December 6, 1967

Over-the-Counter Quotations: Source on request.

Decimals in bid-and-asked and bid change represent 32nds (101.1 means 101 1-32). a-Plus 1-64. b-Yield to call date. c-Certificates of indebtedness. d-Minus 1-64.

Treasury Bonds

				Bid	Asked	Bid Chg.	Yld.
3⅞s,	1968	May		99.6	99.8	...	5.62
3¾s,	1968	Aug.		98.21	99.23	...	5.67
3⅞s,	1968	Nov.		98.12	98.14	...	5.61
2½s,	1963-68	Dec.	●	97.3	97.7	+ .2	5.34
4s,	1969	Feb.		98.2	98.6	+ .1	5.60
2½s,	1964-69	June		95.28	96.0	+ .3	5.27
4s,	1969	Oct.		97.1	97.5	...	5.67
2½s,	1964-69	Dec.	●	94.24	95.0	+ .3	5.14
2½s,	1965-70	Mar.	●	94.4	94.8	+ .2	5.22
4s,	1970	Feb.		96.20	96.24	+ .3	5.60
4s,	1970	Aug.		90.0	96.4	+ .3	5.57
2½s,	1966-71	Mar.	●	91.24	91.28	+ .4	5.24
4s,	1971	Aug.		94.20	94.24	+ .2	5.59
3⅞s,	1971	Nov.		93.26	93.30	+ .4	5.61
4s,	1972	Feb.		93.26	93.30	+ .4	5.65
2½s,	1967-72	June	●	88.20	88.28	+ .6	5.30
4s,	1972	Aug.		93.10	93.18	+ .6	5.58
2½s,	1967-72	Sept.		88.2	88.10	+ .6	5.31
2½s,	1967-72	Dec.		87.12	87.20	+ .6	5.34
4s,	1973	Aug.		91.20	91.28	+ .8	5.69
4⅛s,	1973	Nov.		91.26	92.2	+ .10	5.72
4⅛s,	1974	Feb.	●	91.22	91.30	+ .10	5.69
4¼s,	1974	May		91.28	92.4	+ .8	5.73
3⅞s,	1974	Nov.		89.18	89.26	+ .6	5.67
4s,	1980	Feb.		85.12	85.28	+ .14	5.62
3½s,	1980	Nov.	●	81.8	81.24	+ .18	5.49
3¼s,	1978-83	June		77.14	77.30	+ .18	5.36
3¼s,	1985	May		76.28	77.12	+ .18	5.25
4¼s,	1975-85	May		84.2	84.18	+ .14	5.65
3½s,	1990	Feb.		77.2	77.18	+ .18	5.22
4¼s,	1987-92	Aug.	●	81.18	82.2	+ .16	5.60
4s,	1988-93	Feb.		79.2	79.18	+ .16	5.51
4⅛s,	1989-94	May		79.26	80.10	+ .14	5.55
3s,	1995	Feb.		76.26	77.10	+ .18	4.45
3½s,	1998	Nov.		77.4	77.20	+ .20	4.91

Those that are marked with a (•) are eligible to pay the estate tax. This is only a partial list. The entire list according to circular No. 17 of the Federal Reserve Bank of New York, revised on January 20, 1965, contained as many as 25 different issues.

Note for example, the 3½ (maturity in 1980) were sold at approximately 81.24 or $817.50 per $1,000 bond on December 6, 1967. If purchases prior to death, and part of an estate, it would be valued at par or $1,000 for the payment of the estate tax.

The list may change. Those interested should consult the Treasury Department. Ask for circular No. 300.

In general, U.S. Government Bonds can be purchased and sold on the open market.

Tax-Exempt Bonds

The income from bonds of states and municipalities are exempt from the Federal income tax. This makes them attractive for individuals in high income tax brackets. Some newspapers quote a few bonds. A complete list of tax-exempts are published daily in the "Blue Book." Thousands of issues are included. Those who are interested should examine the Blue Book with their broker.

Tax-exempt bonds fluctuate with the money market the same as all bonds. Those who bought long-term tax-exempts many years ago have suffered significant depreciation of their capital as interest rates rose. It is wise here as in the case of all bonds to *confine yourself to short-term issues only.*

Authority Bonds

These are bonds of states and municipalities, the income from which is tax exempt. However, neither the income nor the principal is guaranteed. Most of them were issued to build toll highways and bridges and factories. Some of them are of excellent quality; others are not. One should not assume that all tax-exempt bonds are guaranteed by their issuing state or municipality. Your broker should be asked to check each one separately. The Blue Book contains a complete list of those that are currently offered. Here is a sampling:

Public Auth. Bonds

	Rate	Mat.	Bid	Ask.
Ashdwn Ark	4¾	'88	89	94
Cal Toll Bdg	3⅞	'92	94¼	95¼
Camd Ind Dev	4⅜	'88	91½	93½
Chelan Distl	5	2013	104½	105½
Ches Br&T	5⅝	2000	71	73
Chgo Cal Sky	3⅜	'95	47	50
Chgo-O'H Intl	4¾	'99	104½	105½
ClintIaIndDev	4.20	'91	97	99
Colum St Pw	3⅞	2003	96¾	97¾
Delaw Tpk	4⅛	2002	100½	102
Doug CPU	4	2018	95¾	96
Eliz RT&B	4½	2000	103	104½
Florida Tpk	4¾	2001	103¼	104¼
Grant CPU 2	3⅞	2005	92½	93½
Grant CPU 2	4⅞	2009	104	105
Gt NOrl Ex	4.90	2006	98½	99½
Illinois Toll	3¾	'95	92¾	93¾
Illinois Toll	4¾	'98	103¼	105
Indiana Toll	3½	'94	85½	86½
JacksonEv x	4	'92	96½	98
JacksonvEx	4.10	2003	96¼	98
Kansas Tpk	3⅝	'94	80	82
Kentucky Tpk	3.40	'94	95	100
Ky Tpke	4¾	2006	101¾	102½
Ky Tpk E	4.80	2000	(z)	(z)
Ky Tpk W	4.85	2000	100	102
Lewispt Bldg	5	'88	97	99
Mackinac Bdg	4	'94	94	98
Maine Tpk	4	'89	97½	99
Maryland B&T	3	'94	9	102
Mary NE Cx	4⅛	2002		103
Mass	A	4¾	'9	106¼
Mas	5	2		92
N		0		1¼
		3		

Convertible Bonds

These bonds are quite popular with institutions and individuals because they combine the relative safety of a bond with the "romance" of common stock. They contain a provision which permits the holder to convert the bond into a definite number of shares of common stock. For example, if a $1,000 bond may be converted into 50 shares of common stock, the bond must rise if the common stock increases above $20 a share. Let us assume that the common stock increases to $30 a share. The bond will have to rise to approximately $1,500 per bond. Standard & Poor issues a book of green sheets for convertible bonds. These can be obtained from your broker. Here is a sample:

CDP[1]   **Cerro de Pasco**   6170
(now Cerro Corp.)
CONVERTIBLE SUBORD. DEB. 5½s, Jan. 1, 1979

Quality Rating	Bond Price	*Shs. Per $1,000 Bd.	*Conv. Price	†Conv. Parity	[1]Stock Price	Stk. Value of Bonds	Invest. Worth	‡Div. Inc.	§Current Return
BB	163	42.68	23.43	38⅛	37	158	90	$68.29	3.38%

*Through December 31, 1968, when the privilege expires. Potential increase in shares to stock outstanding, 9.5%.   †Based on bond price.
‡Per $1,000 bond, based on $1.60 annual dividend; 5% stock dividend paid February 15, 1967.   §Yield to maturity is not relevant.

```
STOCK   20      25      30      35   ▼  40      45      50      55      60      65   STOCK
  |||||||||||||||||||||||||||||||||||||||||||||||||||||||||||||||||||||||||||||||||||
  6170                              S & P CONVERTIBLE BOND PARITY SCALE
  |||||||||||||||||||||||||||||||||||||||||||||||||||||||||||||||||||||||||||||||||||
BOND  80     100     120     140    160▲ 180     200     220     240     260     280  BOND
```

There are two features of convertibles that must be watched.
1. *Callability.* Some bonds may be called at a price not too far from par ($1,000). Those who buy them should be aware of this fact, especially if their purchase price is substantially above par. When a bond is called the holder is usually given sufficient time to convert it to common stock or sell it. If he is on vacation or away from home and his bond is safely tucked away in his vault he may return to discover that he has lost considerably. Those who buy convertible bonds should keep them with their broker or a bank where they can be watched. The Cerro de Pasco bonds may be redeemed by the company at 105 ($1,050 through 1968, then at 103).

2. *Conversion changes and expiration.* The conversion feature of many of these bonds changes every few years. A bond may be convertible into 50 shares of common stock to 1968, then into 45 shares for the next five years, etc., until it expires. The conversion feature of the Cerro bonds expires on December 31, 1968. After that date they will sell as do ordinary 5⅛ % bonds. In 1967 these bonds were selling as high as 189½ ($1,895 for a $1,000 bond). It is dangerous to buy a convertible bond that is so near its expiration date.

Most convertible bonds indicate a conversion price from which one can compute the number of shares into which they can be converted. The method is to divide the par value of the

bond ($1,000) by the conversion price, and the quotient will be
the number of shares that can be obtained. In the case of Cerro,
the conversion price is $23.43. If $1,000 is divided by $23.43
the quotient becomes 42.68. This means that a $1,000 bond
can be converted into 42.68 shares of common stock.

There is an aspect of convertible bonds that investors
discover sooner or later. They can be bought with a small
investment and the balance borrowed from a bank. In some
cases the bank will lend as much as 75% of the value of the
bond. Instead of making $10 for each point that the bond rises,
one makes $40 if a 75% loan is obtained. The reverse is equally
true. The loss becomes $40 instead of $10. Buying convertibles
on margin is a dangerous practice and should be engaged in by
professionals, who can "jump" quickly during adversities.

There are hundreds of convertible bonds that are available.
Every brokerage house can obtain a list for their clients.

One should not rush to buy them hastily. Some are good;
others quite dangerous. The first test is one of quality. This test
will eliminate the marginal companies and bad risks. One should
not be enticed by the high yield and the attractive conversion
feature. When the common drops, the bond loses its glamour.
The second test is the p/e ratio and spread tests. *Buy the
convertible bond only when you would buy the common stock.*
This refers to the better-quality common stocks. If the common
stock is too high to be considered for purchase, the convertible
is also too high. However, if the common is attractive because it
meets the several tests, the convertible bond becomes attractive.

One should be especially careful about buying a convertible
bond at the original date of issue. Most companies time the
issuance of a convertible bond when the common stock is at the
peak of its popularity. A typical example is the convertible
bond of American Machine and Foundry. It is a 4¼% bond
that matures in 1981. It is convertible at $57.46, so that a
$1,000 bond can be converted into 17.4 shares of common
stock. The bond was originally issued by the company in 1961

when the common stock was at the height of its popularity. The common tumbled substantially since then, falling to as low as 13½ in 1966. Those who bought the bond when it was originally issued have suffered quite a loss. Here is a sampling of convertible bonds:

Issue	Conversion Price	No. of Shares Per Bond	July 7, 1967 Ap. Market Price Stock	July 7, 1967 Ap. Market Price Bond
Air Red. 3 7/8-87	$31.25	32.00	$41	$135
Alcoa 5 1/4-91	85.00	11.76	83	119
Alleg. Lud 4-81	52.00	19.23	68	131
Allied Strs. 4 1/2-81	28.00	35.71	33	118
Amer. Airlines 5 1/2-91	61.50	16.26	44	142
Amer. M & F 4 1/4-81	57.46	17.40	23	80
Ampex 5 1/4-91	27.75	36.04	37	142
Armour 4 1/2-83	51.14	19.55	37	98

Convertible Preferred

During the past few years convertible preferred stocks have become popular. Unlike its opposite number in the bond division, it is not a bond, so that the income is not a fixed charge against the company. It is a preferred stock and its dividend has to be voted by the Board of Directors.

Otherwise its convertible feature is similar to the bond. It may be converted into common stock at a predetermined rate. Hence, it will move with the common. Here is an example of a typical convertible preferred stock:

Household Finance
Dividend Rate: $4.40 a share
Convertibility: 3 shares of common for 1 preferred
Dividend Rate on Common: $1.00

The preferred moves with the common because it may be converted into 3 shares of common at any time. In fact, it usually sells at a premium that is more than 3 times the value of the common when the common is selling at a low price because the $4.40 dividend acts as a floor below which the stock will not drop. On July 7, 1967, the common stock closed at $26 ¾ a share and the convertible preferred at $93⅞. It should be noted that there is quite a gap between the price of the common and the preferred. On the basis of 3 shares of common for 1 of preferred, the preferred was worth only 3 times $26¾ or $80. At $93 per share it was selling at a premium of $13. Is it better to buy the preferred or common? The common stock pays $1 a share, making the yield 3½%. The yield on the convertible preferred was 4.7%. If one is interested in a long-term investment he would do better buying the preferred which yields 35% more than the common on an income basis. If and when the common rises the preferred will also increase. The $13 gap will narrow as the common increases.

As in the case of convertible bonds we do not recommend the purchase of these securities on margin.

Income Bonds

There are a few bonds, especially in the railroad division, where the interest is paid only if earned and voted by the Board of Directors. The yield on these bonds is quite high because of the risk. Unlike other bonds they sell "flat," which means that interest is not added to the cost of the bond when it is purchased. Payment on the income bonds of the Central Railroad of New Jersey was suspended in 1967. This ended the large income that their holders were receiving.

Warrants

This is an area of interesting speculation. There are instances where individuals made, or could have made, fortunes.

A warrant is an option which gives the holder the right to buy a stock at a specific price forever, or for a limited period of time.

Example: *Martin Marietta*

There are 195,000 warrants outstanding.

1 warrant plus $45 can buy 2.73 shares of common stock.

The warrants expire on November 1, 1968.

On July 7, 1967, the common closed at approximately $24 a share. The warrant, listed on the American Exchange, closed at approximately $29.

The cost of buying 2.73 shares of common stock was $65.52. One warrant plus $45 buys $65.52 worth of this stock. This makes the warrant worth $20.52 on an exchange basis. The market price of the warrant is $29 or $8.48 more than its worth. What should one do?

If the common meets all the buying tests at this price, the warrants would be worth considering, except for their November 1, 1968, expiration date. *After that date they will be worthless.* This removes the luster from them. The risk is the difference between the market price of 2.73 shares of common stock and $45 because one may convert these warrants into common stock to the very end.

Here are a few warrants with longer expiration dates:

Company	Expiration Date
Trans World Airlines	December 1, 1973
General Acceptance	June 15, 1976
Coburn Credit	August 15, 1979
Textron	May 1, 1984
Allegheny Corp.	Never
Indian Head Mills	May 15, 1990
Investment Corp. America	Never
Tri Continental Corp.	Never

Most people should not buy warrants. No dividends are paid. It represents hope and a lot of prayer. It's a rich-quick idea and leads to more frustration than reward. There have been stories of fabulous fortunes that *others* made.

Rights

Somewhat related to warrants are rights. These are issued to existing stockholders when a company wishes to float a bond or increase the number of shares of stock through a public sale. For example, a company may wish to raise $2½ million by issuing new stock. It has a million shares of common stock outstanding. The stock is currently selling at $30 a share. It may give the existing stockholders the right to subscribe to the new stock at $25 a share, or $5 below the market. It issues 1 million rights, one for each share of stock that is outstanding. One share of stock can be purchased for $25 plus 10 rights. Each right is worth approximately $.50 a share because 10 rights plus $25 equals the $30 which is the value of the common stock on the market. The owner of the common stock may exercise his rights or sell them. They are normally traded on the same exchange as the common stock. There are many individuals who don't want to buy additional common stock and neglect to sell the rights. Remember, if you own stock and obtain rights, either exercise or sell them *before their expiration date.* Millions of dollars are lost by individuals who do neither. Those who buy rights of a company should know they may apply to the underwriter for their share of unsubscribed rights, if any, free of charge. This should be done in advance of the expiration date. This makes it possible to buy the common below the market.

There are individuals who buy rights and subscribe to the stock because they may invest as little as 25% of the value of the stock and borrow the remainder from their broker. This is permitted by law. In other words, they may buy on a 25% margin basis with rights, subject to the individual broker's rules. In general, we do not recommend buying stock on such a skimpy basis. It's the old question of risk and reward.

Options
Puts and Calls

There is another area of investing that is both intriguing and dangerous. It is trading in Puts and Calls.

Calls

A *Call* is a contract that provides that the purchaser of the Call may *buy* from the seller a *given stock* within a limited period of time at a definite price. The buyer pays the seller a certain amount of money for giving him the option. Let us consider an example:

> XYZ Company is selling at $25 a share.
> Terms of Call 6 months.
> Price of Call $25 a share.
> Cost of Call $300.

The buyer of the Call pays the seller $300 immediately.

In return, he receives a contract that states that he *may* buy 100 shares of the XYZ stock at the current market price of $25 a share within the next 6 months. He is not compelled to buy the stock.

If he fails to buy the stock *within* the contract period he forfeits the $300.

If he exercises his option he buys the stock at $25 per share or $2,500 for 100 shares, plus brokerage commissions. He *receives all dividends* that accrued to the stock during the option period. His cost will be $2,800 plus brokerage commission less accumulated dividends.

He will not exercise his option if the stock is selling below $25.

Normally, he will exercise it if the stock is selling sufficiently above $25 to cover his cost plus commissions and transfer taxes.

Calls are purchased by individuals who have reason to believe that the stock will rise sufficiently within the time limit to make a profit. Sometimes, they have special information about a security. Instead of making an investment of $2,500 for 100 shares as required in the example cited above, they invest only $300. If their judgment is wrong their loss is limited to that amount only.

Normally, Calls are traded on the most active securities. If the security rises sufficiently, they exercise the Call or sell it at a higher price to another buyer. Calls may be sold or exercised within the time limit.

There is an aspect of this operation that is worthy of serious investor attention.

Sell Calls on securities that you would otherwise buy.

Assume that you have investigated the XYZ Company and have decided that it meets all your tests and that you would like to buy it. If you can, sell a Call on this security for six months or longer. *But, make sure you buy the stock simultaneously.* By purchasing the stock you remove the risk if the stock rises as it should, if you researched carefully. If you sell a $2,500 Call for $300 your cash investment is only $2,200. Considering buying and selling commissions should the Call be exercised, you can make as much as $250 on a cash outlay of $2,200 for six months. This represents an annual yield of 23%. If the Call is not exercised you keep the $300.

The danger in selling Calls is that there is a temptation to sell those on securities that are highly priced, a kind of short selling. This places the seller on the other side of the gamble. If one can discipline himself to selling Calls only on stock that *he would buy*, he can do well.

If you sell an option and buy the stock you will have to keep it for the duration of the Call period. In essence you will be "frozen," for the life of the Call.

Puts

Like Calls, *Puts* represent an investment in options.

A *Put* is a contract that provides that the purchaser of the Put may *sell* to the seller a *given stock* at a *given price* within a limited period time. For this privilege the buyer pays the seller a certain amount of money. For example:

XYZ Company stock is selling for $25 a share.
Terms of Put 6 months.

Price of Put $25 a share.
Option money $300.

The buyer of the Put gives the seller $300.

The contract provides that he may sell to the seller of the Put 100 shares of stock at $25 a share, or $2,500 for 100 shares, during the time limit, 6 months.

The buyer of the Put hopes or expects the stock to drop sufficiently below $2,200 to enable him to sell the stock to the seller of the Put and make a profit. Assume that the stock drops to $18 a share he makes quite a profit.

The buyer of the Put makes money only if the stock drops in price. If it rises he loses his option money. This is the most he can lose.

Our advice as in the case of Calls is: *Be a seller only. Sell Puts only on those stocks that you would otherwise buy.*

Assume you would like to buy the XYZ stock mentioned above. If you sell a Put *don't buy the stock.*

One of two things must take place:

1. *The stock goes up.* The buyer of the Put will not exercise it and the seller will keep the option money.

2. *The stock goes down.* The buyer of the Put exercises his option. The cost to the seller of the Put will be the agreed-on price, minus the option money of $300. Thus, the stock will cost not $2,500 but only $2,200. In effect, the seller of the Put buys the stock at a lower price.

Straddles

A combination of a *Put* and a *Call* is a *Straddle.*

A Straddle is a contract that provides that the buyer of the Straddle may *either buy or sell* to the seller a *given stock* at a *given price* for a *limited period of time.* For this privilege the buyer pays the seller a certain amount of money. For example:

XYZ Company stock is selling for $25 a share.

Terms of Straddle 6 months.
Price of Straddle $25 a share.
Cost of Straddle $500.

The buyer of the Straddle gives the seller $500.

During the next 6 months he may buy or sell 100 shares of stock to the seller of the Straddle for $25 a share. He pays a large amount for this double privilege.

The probability is that the buyer of the Straddle will exercise his option because most securities move either up or down. This does not mean that he will profit from his venture. He will make a profit only if the stock rises or falls by more than $500 plus the brokerage commission that he will have to pay. If the security moves up or down by any reasonable amount, he will exercise his option, if only to reduce his losses.

As with Puts and Calls, *only a seller be.*

Sell a Straddle only on a stock that you own or on a stock of which you don't mind owning 200 shares.

In the example previously cited, if a Straddle is sold for $500, the stock should be purchased to protect the Call. If the stock rises sufficiently, the buyer of the Straddle will exercise his option and obtain the stock. If it drops sufficiently the buyer of the Straddle will exercise the option by selling the stock at $25 per share or $2,500 for 100 shares. In that case, the seller of the Straddle will own 200 shares of stock.

Summary of Puts, Calls or Straddles

Those who want to deal in options should be *sellers only.*

There are other forms of options that represent complete gambling and should not be considered. Those who are interested should read books on the subject.

There are income tax aspects of options that should interest investors. Under certain conditions the sale of long-term calls could result in long-term capital gains. Your accountant should be consulted on this matter.

Newspapers and periodicals normally contain ads of Puts, Calls, and Straddles. Here are samples:

Oct. 20, 1967

SPECIAL put OPTIONS

PER 100 SHARES:

close					
35⅜	Beryllium	38	Dec.	14	$425.00
85⅞	General Motors .	84½	Dec.	18	350.00
55½	Gulf & Western .	56⅜	Dec.	22	425.00
85⅞	Fairchild Camera	88⅝	Dec.	21	950.00
133½	Eastman Kodak .	135	Dec.	14	650.00
47⅝	Comsat	52	Apr.	19	850.00
63	Gen'l Dynamics	61¾	Dec.	27	350.00
76⅛	Westinghouse El.	77¼	Dec.	14	500.00
68⅝	Genl. Prec. Eq.	71⅜	Dec.	14	650.00
27⅝	Elco Corp. ...	28¼	Jan.	16	350.00
41⅞	Sprague Ele'		Nov.	29	275.00
53⅞	Longines W		Dec.	18	750.00
49⅝	SCM Cor'		'ec.	21	650.00
22¾	Natl. U			29	300.00
47⅛	Weste			14	350.00
46	Eas'				500.00
29¾	Fl				350.00
25½					'75.00
35¾					00
2?					

Nov. 27, 1967

SPECIAL CALL OPTIONS

Per 100 Shares **Plus Tax**

close					
25¼	Aerojet General	25⅞	Feb.	9	$262.50
33¾	Chromalloy	33⅞	Jan.	19	325.00
21⅛	Commonwlth. Oil	21⅜	Feb.	26	250.00
75½	Data Proc. F & G	74	Jan.	29	987.50
29¾	Dixilyn	27⅞	Feb.	20	525.00
52	Dome Petroleum	52¾	Feb.	27	625.00
56½	E G & G	56	Feb.	27	687.50
47⅝	Engelhardt Ind.	43½	Aug.	26	1050.00
27½	Flying Tiger	27¾	Jan.	29	287.50
28⅞	Globe Union	28	Mar.	11	475.00
62	Hilton Hotels ...		Feb.	12	950.00
50¼	Longine Wittn		'n.	8	437.50
48⅛	Mattel ...				525.00
21	Nation'				'5.00
36⅝	No'				
24					

Nov. 27, 1967

WE ARE BIDDING FOR THE FOLLOWING

STRADDLES

AT THE MARKET	65 days	95 days
Amer. Airlines	$300.00	$400.00
Beckman Instru. Inc.	650.00	850.00
Belco Petrol.	550.00	700.00
Burroughs Corp.	1200.00	1600.00
Collins Radio	1100.00	1500.00
Continental Airl.	300.00	400.00
Control Data	1900.00	2500.00
Dixilyn Corp.	400.00	525.00
Dynalectron C ..	450.00	600.00
Electronic A	400.00	550.00
Flying Tig'	'0.00	400.00
Gulf & W		750.00
Mattel		750.00
McDor		625.00
Mono		00
Per'		
Sc'		

Short-Term Money

Large organizations and institutions with significant amounts of money that normally lie idle for as little as six days should become familiar with the operation of the "money market." There are large, well-established finance, credit, small loan companies, and factoring establishments that are continuously borrowing money at current rates of interest. The going rate in mid-July 1967 was 4⅝% for 15-day money. Here are a few large borrowers:

> Ford Motor Credit Co.
> Montgomery Ward Credit Co.
> General Motors Credit Corp.
> J. C. Penny Credit Corp.

A few telephone calls and some research will reveal many more.

Other Areas of Investment

This book has limited itself to securities. There are other areas of investment that will be mentioned briefly.

Real estate

This is an excellent area, limited to those who can devote their time to management or who are able to retain professionals. The small investor is handicapped because he is forced to place his limited funds in the hands of individuals or small organizations whom he does not know. Some are competent, others not; some honest, others not. There are very few national organizations with long-established records that can be studied. Most realty organizations in which small investors can participate have no past record that can be used as a guide. As a result the risk is great. A case in point are the realty syndications that mushroomed after the last world war. They promised 10% and more, tax free. For a period of years they did quite well. When the collapse came billions of dollars were lost.

Stamps, coins, antiques, art, etc.

There are individuals who have done quite well saving stamps or coins. The hobby can be enjoyable and profitable. A great deal of time is required. Time and an affluent society have made these valuable.

Antiques have multiplied in value during the past few decades because time has made them scarce and an affluent society, valuable. Care must be taken against fakes, which are increasing in numbers.

Art, likewise, has become more valuable with the years. Fakes are increasing. The general rule is that if the price is too low it will probably be a fake.

It should be noted that there is an estate aspect involved in the purchase of antiques and art. These are part of the taxable estate. If they cannot be sold readily they could become a burden to the beneficiaries. They should be purchased with the estate problem in mind. Covering life insurance, sufficient to pay the estate tax, should be purchased.

Summary of Chapter

There are many areas of investment, some relatively safe, others quite dangerous.

In general one should not seek investment where the rewards are larger than the norm. Therein lurk the hidden dangers. If the current rate on high-grade bonds is 5%, one that yields 7% usually contains some flaw in it. It is enticing—so are poisoned berries.

Do not seek bizarre situations for investment. If you look hard enough they will find you. There are styles in investing as elsewhere. At one period realty syndications captured the imagination by their large tax-exempt yield. It ended as most do, in disaster. At another period, such as in 1962, it was new issues, which were bought at $4 per share in the morning and sold for $8 in the afternoon. This, too, enjoyed its spree and collapsed. At one time large amounts were invested in Florida orange groves until a frost ended that. Drilling oil wells, buying pedigree bulls and cows, and horse racing are other forms of investments. Their lure is to transform current income to long-term capital gains and so save on income taxes. These involve the normal risks of business, compounded by the human factor of integrity. In dealing with large established corporations there is a risk, but it is much less than that incurred with smaller ones.

There is a difference between large investors and small ones. The large investor can afford to hire experts in oil drilling, cattle breeding, art, etc., and protect himself. The small investor cannot. He must therefore limit himself to investments that are suitable for him. Those who stray usually get hurt. Those who invest for a fair and modest return usually do better.

7
This and That

There are numerous technical matters which the investor should understand to avoid friction. Some beginners, for example, object to the questions they have to answer to make a purchase of stock. The fact is that an account has to be opened to buy even one little share of stock. This is a requirement of the New York Stock Exchange and no doubt of most exchanges. In this chapter we will present several items that should be known by both investors and traders. The New York Stock Exchange has pamphlets on specific items.

Opening an Account

The New York Stock Exchange as well as other exchanges requires that an account be opened before an order is placed. The procedure is to answer a few questions, including the name of the bank with which the person deals. There are many ways of opening an account. Here is a partial list:

1. Individual account. An individual, over twenty-one, may open an account in his name.

2. Joint account with right of survivorship. Husband and wife may open a joint account with the right of survivorship. In this type of account, should one spouse pass away the securities will belong to the survivor. This does not mean that the state rules can be bypassed as far as transfer is concerned. Nor does it mean that the estate tax laws will not apply. Both have to be taken into consideration. However, the transfer is easier.

3. Partnerships and Tenants in Common accounts. Club accounts.

4. Corporate Trust and Fiduciary accounts.

5. Profit-Sharing Plan accounts.

6. Custodian accounts for minors. In these accounts, the security belongs to the minor. The adult acts only as the custodian. He cannot appropriate the funds or income for his own use. The custodian should not use his own Social Security number but should obtain a special identification number for this account. In corporation, trust and special accounts the broker will normally ask for supporting papers.

Power of Attorney

An investor may designate another to manage his account. He signs a limited or unlimited power of attorney.

A limited power of attorney restricts the person who operates the account to buying and selling stock on behalf of the principal.

An unlimited power of attorney gives the operator the right to withdraw money and securities.

Except for intimate members of the same family, only a limited power of attorney should be given. The only exception might be to a bank or trust company which is insured against larceny.

Cash Account

In such an account the customer agrees to pay cash for all his purchases. The money is due four business days after the purchase has been made. If payment is made after that day the broker must charge interest on the money due.

Margin Account

In such an account the customer invests part of the total cost of the security and borrows the balance from the broker. The amount he may borrow varies with the margin requirements set by the Federal Reserve Board and additional restrictions by his broker. Since November 6, 1963, the margin requirement has been 70%. This means that at least 70% of the cost of the stock has to be paid by the customer and the balance borrowed from the broker. There are exceptions where customers were on a lower margin basis prior to November 6, 1963.

Where a customer buys stock through the exercise of rights the margin requirements may be as little as 25%. A broker may require a larger investment. When a customer opens a margin account he has to give the broker the right to lend the unpaid portion of his stock.

Where to Keep Securities

Those who buy securities on margin have no choice. They must keep them with the broker as collateral for the loan.

Those who buy for cash may keep their securities with the broker or they may have the stock registered in their name and mailed to them. They may also have the stock registered in their name and kept with the broker.

If the stock is registered in the client's name he will receive dividends and communications from the company. However, if it is registered in "street" name the broker collects the dividends and deposits it in the customer's account or mails it to him as he wishes. "Street" name means that the stock is registered in the name of the broker. When the certificate reaches the latter, the client's name is attached to it so that the broker knows who the owner is.

If the client has the stock sent to his home he should place it in his vault. If it is lost he will have to replace it. This is quite costly.

It is advisable to keep securities with members of the New York Stock Exchange. They will collect dividends and follow up failures and delays. They are quite safe. The Exchange has a $10 million blanket bond covering employees' fraud and a $25 million reserve for contingencies. In addition they are member firms carefully supervised and inspected regularly.

Keeping securities in street name has another advantage. In

case of death the transfers are made more expeditiously. Where the securities are in the name of the deceased, waivers may have to be received from many states and even foreign countries. All this is avoided if they are in street name.

Odd and Round Lots

Most stocks sell in lots of 100 shares. This is called a *round lot*. There are a few inactive stocks where the round lot unit is 10 shares.

Where the unit of trading is 100 shares, an order to buy or sell from 1 to 99 shares is called an *odd lot*. Where the unit is 10 shares, an odd lot is from 1 to 9 shares.

Cost of Odd Lots

The purchaser of an odd lot has to pay an additional $.12½ per share or ⅛th of a point if the price of the stock is less than $55 a share, and $.25 or ¼ of a point if it is $55 or more. If he is the seller he loses ⅛ or ¼ point. The odd lot charge goes to the "Odd Lot" dealer and not to the broker. The latter charges the regular commission.

The odd lot differential is charged because the Odd Lot dealers must execute all buy and sell orders when offered and perforce must keep inventory at all times. Normally, a broker has no inventory. He is simply an agent between a buyer and seller.

Execution of Odd Lots

Odd lots are executed at the very next round lot sale if the order is placed at the market, or when the differential is sufficient to accommodate the price, if the order is placed at a given price. If the customer's order is placed before the market opens and is a market order, the customer will get the opening price plus or minus the differential depending whether he is a buyer or seller. If the order is placed during the day and is a market order, the customer will receive the very next price, plus or minus the differential, at which a round lot is traded, provided approximately 3 minutes elapsed since the order was placed. It takes that much time for the order to reach the Odd Lot dealer. Disputes sometimes arise because the customer thinks he has been given a higher price than is warranted. He should ask his Registered Representative (RR) to check the exact time the order was placed and the official time of the floor executions of the round lot after that. Errors are made, especially in an active stock, where half a dozen trades may occur within a minute. Unless there is great urgency to buy at the market, buying at a price will result in fewer arguments.

If an odd lot order is placed at a limited price, that is the most he can be charged. Therefore the stock has to rise by the differential if he is a seller or fall by that amount if he is a buyer. For example, if the order is to buy an odd lot at $35 a share, the stock must drop to $34\frac{7}{8}$. If the stock does not drop to $34\frac{7}{8}$ the purchase will not be made. Arguments often arise because the customer notes that the newspaper indicates that the low of the day was $35 and he did not receive his stock. The dispute becomes especially intense should the stock close at a higher price.

How to Place an Order for a Round Lot
There are normally three ways to place an order.

1. At the market.
2. At a definite price.
3. At a definite price-stop.

Before discussing this subject, it is important to understand the mechanics involved in executing an order on the New York Stock Exchange. To facilitate the execution of orders the floor of the Exchange is subdivived into areas, called *Trading Posts*. There are 18 of these. Every security is traded around one of them. For example, U.S. Steel is traded at Post 2 and Standard Oil of New Jersey is at Post 9. If an order calls for buying or selling U.S. Steel the broker goes to Post 2 where he will meet other brokers who also have buy or sell orders. In addition, he will meet one or two specialists who are in charge of making an orderly market in the stock.

Buying and selling securities represents a continuous series of auctions. The specialist starts by making the "market" 44-$\frac{1}{4}$. The first number 44 is the bid price at which he will buy 100 shares of stock. The second, 44$\frac{1}{4}$, is the ask or offering price, at which he will sell 100 shares. Any broker "in the crowd" may announce another bid or asking price. For example, he might make the market 44$\frac{1}{8}$ bid. This means that he will buy 100 shares for 44$\frac{1}{8}$. Or he might make the offering price 44$\frac{3}{8}$. This means he is willing to pay 44$\frac{3}{8}$ for 100 shares. If the order is to buy the stock the broker will naturally select the lowest offering price or if it is a sell order he will take the highest bid price. When the brokers representing buyers and sellers have completed a transaction a new auction is started and a new bid and ask price is posted. It may be the same as the previous one or it may be different. For example, the last trade may have been made at 44$\frac{1}{8}$. The new market may be 44$\frac{1}{8}$-$\frac{3}{8}$. Normally, when a stock is in great demand the bids and offerings keep pushing upward. When there are more anxious sellers than buyers they keep sliding down.

Using the modern electronic devices that can be found in most brokerage houses, the bid and ask prices are posted with every trade. When the appropriate button is pushed on the electronic machine, the last trade is given as well as the new bid and ask quotes. Example (X is the symbol for U.S. Steel):

X

L 44$\frac{1}{8}$ (last price)

B 44$\frac{1}{8}$ (new bid)

A44$\frac{3}{8}$ (new ask)

Subject to normal human error, the new auction is for 44 $\frac{1}{8}$ bid and 44$\frac{3}{8}$ ask. Trouble starts when the stock becomes active. It is at that time that neither figure can be relied upon. By the time the order reaches the post the market may have changed several times. In a rising market the 44$\frac{3}{8}$ offer may vanish in a matter of seconds. By the time the order reaches the floor, the market may be 44⅝ -¾. The person who bid 44⅜ originally is naturally disturbed and angry at "someone" when he "loses" the stock. Or the seller may be upset if his security drops significantly below his 44⅛ bid price. It should be remembered that in an active market there are usually many buyers and sellers competing against each other. If a person has a grievance he can take his case to the Board of Governors of the New York Stock Exchange.

How anxious should one be when the stock he wishes to buy is rising rapidly? Our advice is, *stay cool.* When a stock is in great demand, prices keep rising to meet the demand of anxious buyers. After a while sellers come in and the price falls back.

With this in mind, consider the three ways of placing an order:

1. In a market order the buyer will pay the lowest offering price available at the time his floor broker reaches the trading post. If it is a market order to sell he will receive the highest bid price.

2. If the order is placed at a definite price, his floor broker will take it to the post and try to execute it. However, if the order is "away" from the market he will leave it with the specialist, who will record it in his little black book and execute it if a buyer or seller appears during the day to meet that price.

3. If the order is given at a price followed by the word stop, the broker will leave it with the specialist who will record it that way in his black book at the appropriate price. If the stock reaches that price, it becomes an order to buy or sell at the market. For example, assume that a stock is selling at $55 a share. A customer wishing to limit his risk should the stock fall places his order to sell it at *$53 stop.* This means that he wants the order changed to a market order should it fall to $53 a share. He will sell at the very next trade regardless of the price.

Placing stop loss orders is a dangerous practice because there may be other like-minded individuals who also placed stop loss orders at 53. What would happen if 5,000 share orders were placed at or near this price? The avalanche might drop the stock

to 52 or even less. Stop loss orders could play havoc with prices
in a bad market. That is why the Exchange bans them from
time to time.

Several years ago a book was written on how to "make a
fortune" in the market by placing stop loss orders several points
below the market as soon as a security was purchased. Like
other fads this one lasted long enough to wreck a few fortunes.
The only one who made money was the author of the book,
who probably recouped his own trading losses by turning
author.

Unless otherwise stated, an order expires at the end of the
business day. If the customer wants it extended, he should so
state clearly to his RR when he places his order. He should
specify: good for a week, month, etc., or Good Till Cancelled
(GTC), as he wishes.

Selling Short

It is easy to understand buying or selling stock. Selling short
often confuses people, because the sale is made by a person who
does not own the security. In securities you can sell first and
buy later or buy first and sell later. They are interchangeable. In
other words, you can sell U.S. Steel even if you don't own it.
Your broker will lend you the stock (if he has it or can borrow
it) for delivery to the person who bought it from you. The
broker will ask you to deposit sufficient funds as if you bought
the stock on margin. (Under rules in effect in 1967 it was 70%
of the value of the stock.) At some time you must "cover" your
sale, that is purchase the stock. If you buy the stock at a lower
price you will make money. However, if the purchase is made at
a higher price you will lose money. When a dividend is declared
on the stock *the short seller has to pay it*.

Short selling cannot be used by professionals to drive prices
down because a short sale can only be made on an "up tick."
This means that the stock must rise by at least ⅛ of a point
from the previous trade for the short sale. For example, assume
a person wants to sell 100 shares of stock at $44 a share when it

is selling at 44. He places his order thus: "Sell X at 44 short" (he must specify *short*). If the stock sells at 44 for the next twenty sales, the short sale will not be completed. However, if the stock drops to 43⅞ then rises to 44 his sale of 100 shares will be executed.

Short selling is a dangerous practice and should not be attempted by the average person. It is strictly a professional operation. Most people yearn to sell a stock short, usually after they have sold their own, and it continues to rise. It represents a blow to their ego. They seek revenge by wanting to sell it short, just to prove to themselves that their judgment was sound when they sold the security. The fact is they may be right and the stock may be too high, earnings considered. However, years may elapse before a correction takes place. By that time their limited funds and patience will both be exhausted. This is an operation for the professional, who if he is wrong will take his loss quickly.

Short selling against the box merits understanding. In this case the stock is sold short, but the person owns the stock. He sells short to transfer his gain from one year to another. Assume a person has a gain of $3,000 in a security. The month is November. He is in a high income tax bracket and has already made a substantial amount of money. He wishes to defer taking the profit to the following year. He sells it short, giving his broker his stock as collateral. The next year he delivers his stock to "cover" his short sale. The profit takes place when the transaction has been completed. The proceeds cannot be used to buy another security. It is "frozen" for the period of the sale.

Buying Calls to Protect Short Sales,

For a trader who sells fast-moving stock short, buying a Call on the security to be sold short is advisable. The premium for the Call represents insurance against too large a loss on the short sale. For example, a security is selling for $50 a share. A trader wants to sell the stock short. He sells the stock short and simultaneously buys a six-month Call at the same price, paying a premium of $500. If the stock drops significantly, as he expected, his profit will be reduced by the $500 he paid for the Call. If the stock rises significantly (as happens quite often) he will lose on the short sale, but gain on the Call. In this way he will limit his loss to approximately $500 plus several commissions. This operation is not recommended for the average person.

On the 20th of each month the New York and American Stock Exchange publish a list of securities which have large short interests. The following is a partial list:

Big Board Short Interest Eased To 14,888,812 Shares at June 15

	6-15-67	5-15-67	Shares Listed
Abbott Laboratories	2,904	5,500	13,362,538
ABC Consolidated	4,400	1,309	3,184,064
Addressograph-Multig	11,835	33,123	8,030,506
Admiral Corp	164,057	139,637	5,119,722
Air Products & Chem	20,752	17,366	4,635,479
Air Reduction	r22,398	s21,056	10,750,566
Alberto-Culver	8,320	13,080	3,027,491
Alleghany Corp	5,724	3,975	6,875,673
Allegheny Ludlum	11,925	12,511	4,491,692
Allied Chemical	3,775	7,071	28,444,678
Allied Stores	890	4,370	7,308,634
Allis-Chalmers Mfg	7,610	8,816	9,466,167
Alpha Portlnd Cement	5,020	4,920	1,843,913
Amerada Petroleum	5,185	4,385	14,753,200
American Air Filter	8,755	9,215	1,828,648
Amer Airlines	68,906	18,435	9,433,985
Amer Bosch Arma	11,499	8,337	1,946,991
Amer Cyanamid	5,605	8,376	44,690,608
Amer Enka	5,525	3,700	5,421,792
Am Exp Isbrandtsn	3,690	1,258	1,488,272
Amer Home Products	r13,826	s10,149	49,426,625
Amer Hospital Supply	32,362	23,414	9,298,914
Amer Machine & Fdry	6,894	5,653	17,253,989
Amer Motors	237,199	194,086	19,268,359
Amer News	3,542	242	1,828,303
Amer Photocopy Equip	58,860	67,759	8,006,450
Amer Research & Dev	9,510	8,253	1,550,000
Ame So Africa ɔv	6,716	6,202	2,400,000
Am̃ ɪn-Standʑ	⸱724	9,345	11,709,936
A ꞁephonc ꞁel	⸱82	65,422	539,673,372
Zinc	3	5,812	1,371,034
⋯⋯	⋯⋯⋯	65,818	9,530,997
⋯⋯	⋯⋯	2,3	2,992,761
⋯⋯	⋯⋯	⸱9	912,240
⋯⋯			9,3ʄ
			2

No Trade

There is an aspect of market procedure that can easily frighten a beginner. He buys an inactive stock and watches it go up and down. Then one day it disappears. He thinks of the worst. He is mistaken.

Each day there are a number of securities that do not trade because the buyers and sellers did not get together. The *Wall Street Journal* and other newspapers publish those securities thus neglected.

N.Y. Stock Exchange

Closing Bid and Asked Prices of Stocks Not Traded

	Bid	Asked
Abacus	15¼	15⅜
Alleg West	102	106
Am Bk Note	22½	23¼
Am Bk N pf	63¼	65
AExIsbrn pf	80½	82¼
AmInvest pf	89	90½
Am MFd pf	81	82½
AmStand pf	134	137
AmWWk 5pf	20⅝	21¼
Anch HG pf	83¼	85½
ArmstCk pf	74½	76½
Ashl Oil pf	63¼	64
AtlCityEl pf	77½	79
Aust Nich	25½	25¾
Aust N pf	60	62
Basic Inc pf	45	47
Bath Ind wi	14¾	15
BeckShoe pf	89	91¾
Beech Crk	35	36
BeechLS pf	54	54⅜
BenF 4.50pf	73	74½
BenF 4.30pf	75¼	76
BenFin pfV	40½	41
Bond Strs	20½	21
BorgW pf	79¾	81½
Brwn Shoe	67⅝	68
CampRed fn	16	22
Can Dry pf	77⅛	79
Can Sou Ry	60	61½
Canad Brew	6⅞	7
CanBrew fn	6¾	8⅛
Canal Rand	15¾	16
arrier Gen	28¼	28½
Case pf A	23⅝	24
Celan 7 pf	124	127
Cent Aguirr	38	38¼
Ches Cp Va	34	34½
CinGE pfB	89½	90½
CIT Fin 5pf	88	90
Clev Pitts	60½	62
Cluett P pf	124½	130
ColgPalm pf	68½	69½
Col Pict pf	90	91
Coml Cr pf	75½	77
Coml Sol pf	26¾	27¾
ConEdis pfC	79½	82
CnPw 4.52pf	85	86¼
CnPw 4.16	77	7
Cont B	95½	
Cont	75¾	
Cor	19¼	
	77	
Jewel Co pf	73½	76½
JimWalt 5pf	15½	15¾
Kaiser 59pf	110¼	112
Kaiser 66pf	116	117
Kaiser nc pf	43	43¾
KCPL 4.50pf	82	84
KCPL 4.35pf	78	83
KCPL 4.20pf	76	77½
KCPL 4 pf	75	80
Lanvin pf	44½	45½
Ligg My pf	126	129
Ling TVt 3pf	185	192¾
Ltton cv3pf	213	220
LoneStCe pf	86	87¼
LongILt pfD	75¼	79½
LongILt pfE	75	79
Lorillard pf	125	127
Manh Shirt	21¼	21½
MasseyF fn	20⅝	21
May 1945 pf	71	73
May 1947 pf	71	73½
May 1959 pf	71¼	73
May 3.40 pf	62	66
May 1.80 pf	34	35
McCro pf B	62	63
McCro pf D	83½	85
McQuay No	19⅝	19⅞
Mead 4.25pf	83⅝	85
Mercant Str•	36	36⅛
Merck pf	70⅜	71½
MetE 3.90pf	69	71
MetE 3.85pf	68½	72
MetE 3.80pf	67½	69½
Mich GasUt	21¼	21½
MidlRo pfA	147	152
Mo Pac RR	79	79⅞
Moh 4.20pf	80	82
Moh 3.50pf	69	72
NDist 4.25pf	81⅝	82¾
Nat Sug Ref	15¾	16¼
Neisner	9¼	9½
Newberry pf	61⅛	62
NJ PwLt pf	71¼	73
Newmont pf	141	150
NiaM 4.10pf	72¼	75
NiaM 3.90pf	66	67
Nor Central	69	70
NoNG 5.80pf	98	99
NSPw 4.56pf	92	85
NSPw 4.16		7
SPw 4.		
Pw		
Pw		

American Stock Exch.

Closing Bid and Asked Prices of Stocks Not Traded

	Bid	Asked
A K U	38½	40½
Ala Pow pf	74	75½
Alan Wood	24½	25
Alan Wd pf	74	75
AlliedArt pf	9½	10
Alcoa pf	70½	71½
AmThrd pf	5⅞	6⅛
Ark PL pf	84¼	84⅞
Assd ElInd	.5	5⅝
AVC Corp	95	105
Baldwin Sec	5½	5¾
Bickfords	15½	15⅞
Binney & S	36	36½
Bloss Hydra	.4¾	5
Bohack HC	17⅝	17¾
Bohack pf	67¼	69
Brandyw	24¼	24½
BritAm Tob	10⅜	10⅝
BritAmTb r	10⅜	11
Brown F A	25	25½
Brown F pf	6⅝	6¾
Byers Co	10¾	10⅞
Cdn Int Pw	34½	35
Cdn Prop	7¾	7¾
Cen Sec pfB	42½	45
CenSec pfC	25½	26¼
Coburn pfB	26¼	26½
Corroon Rey	18¾	19¼
Crowley Mil	12½	13
Crystal Oil	6¼	6½
Dist Ltd	2⅝	2⅞
Dom Brdge	17½	19½
Dom StCoal	7⅞	8
Domin Text	17	24
Domtar	15	15¼
Dunlop Ltd	4¼	4 7-16
East A Dev	7⅞	8¼
Eastern Co	33⅞	34½
Emenee	3⅜	3½
EmpDEl pf	84½	86
Esq RadE	8	8⅛
Fst N Rlt pf	7⅝	7⅞
FstN Rl wt	⅜	½
Fishman	12⅞	13
Forest City	5⅜	5½
Gen El Ltd	6¾	7
Ga Pow 5pf	87	90
Griesedk	14¾	15¼
Groc StrPd	25¾	26¼
Harveys Str	7⅛	7⅜
HellerWE pf	88	90
HellerW 4pf	65	67½
Higbie M	22⅝	22⅞
ImpTh	9¼	9 15-1
Imp	13⅛	1
	⅜	
Marco Int	5⅞	6⅛
Maule Ind	4¾	5
Merch Refr	26½	27
Mich Chem	25¾	26
Midw Inves	17	20
Minn PL pf	86½	87½
Molybden pf	64	65½
MonPw pfA	77	79
MonPw pfB	86½	88½
MonPw pfC	78	80
Mont Wd A	123½	125½
Murray Oh	28½	29
NY Auction	24¾	25¼
NoIndPS pf	74	74½
Overs Sec	19½	20
Pac Cst 6pf	22¾	23⅛
PGE 5pf	21⅞	22¼
P Ltg 4.40pf	75½	78½
P Ltg 4.36pf	73½	74¾
Pantasote	6⅝	6⅞
Parvin Doh	12¼	12¾
Parv Doh pf	51½	53½
Penn Traff	14⅝	14⅞
Pep Boys	14¼	14½
PitDe Moine	28¼	28¾
Pit Lake E	116½	118½
PlymRub B	11¾	12
Prairie Oil	3½	3 11-16
PresReal A	9¾	10⅛
Provid Gas	11⅝	11¾
PuerRic Tel	96	97¼
Quality Imp	21	21⅛
St Law Cp	20	20¼
San Carlos	6⅝	6⅞
S Die 4.40pf	15⅝	16¼
SimmBrd pf	20½	21½
SCE org pf	33½	34½
SCE 4.78 pf	20⅝	21¼
South Royal	42	42¼
StAllian pfA	125	129
StdDredg pf	22½	23
Std Mot A	9⅞	10
Std Product	23⅛	23⅜
Steel Co Can	21¼	21¾
TastyBak A	19¼	19¾
TexPw Lt pf	80½	81
Tob Secur	3⅜	3½
Tob Secur D	9 1-16	9¾
ToledoEd pf	71¼	72
TransInv pf	10	10¼
Triangl Pac	6⅛	6⅜
U Invest	13¼	13½
Yd Om	16	17
Bnd pf		3
rth		½
pf		

Reading a Newspaper

There is much financial news in almost every newspaper. If read carefully it will enrich one's understanding of our economy, world trends and events.

An intensive study of this important subject cannot be made in this short section. Books have been written on it. Careful day-by-day reading of the financial pages is advisable. The rewards in understanding and profit will be most satisfying.

General News

Most companies publish their financial reports periodically, most of them on a quarterly basis. Therein are summarized their sales and profits. Those who are interested should write to the company for more complete reports.

Articles appear regularly on the cost of living, interest rates, Federal Reserve and government policies, all of which affect securities. For example, the $10 billion Federal deficit of 1966-67 caused a serious strain on the availability of money and forced interest rates to soar to unprecedented heights. In addition, corporate changes, flow of gold, and a host of items appear, each important to the national picture.

Specific Items

Each day the morning newspapers report the transactions that took place the previous day. Here is a typical section:

Dec. 6, 1967

A-B-C

--1967--				Sales in					Net
High	Low	Stocks	Div.	100s	Open	High	Low	Close	Chg.
17⅞	13	Abacus	.70f	14	16¾	16⅞	16⅝	16⅝	– ¼
53⅞	41	Abbott Lab	1	31	44½	45	44½	45	+ ¼
34⅞	27⅞	Abex Cp	1.60	8	29½	29½	29¼	29¼	.....
58¼	38⅛	ACF Ind	2.20	55	45	45¼	44⅜	44⅜	– ⅜
46¾	32	Acme Mkt	2b	55	33	33⅛	32⅜	32⅜	– ⅛
33⅜	27	AdamE	2.41g	29	33⅜	33⅜	32¾	32¾	– ½
87¼	14½	AdMillis	.40a	77	65	67½	64¾	65⅝	+1⅛
75½	46⅞	Address	1.40	112	73	73½	72	73⅛	+ ⅜
38	18⅛	Admiral	.25p	162	18½	19	18⅛	19	+ ⅝
69⅛	35	Aeroquip	1b	7	67½	67½	67⅛	67⅛	.....
46¼	31⅝	Air Prod	.20b	34	38½	38½	38⅛	38⅜	– ⅛

Reading from left to right:

1. *1967 High Low.* In this column the highest and lowest prices at which the securities sold this year are indicated. During the first few months it includes the previous year as well.

Example: Up to December 1967 at least 100 shares of Abbott Laboratory were sold for as low as 41 and as high as 53⅞.

2. *Name of Company and Regular Dividend.* Herein are the name of the company and the regular annual dividend that it pays. The dates of payment can be found by referring to the Standard & Poor report.

3. *Sales in 100s.* This column indicates the number of shares that were traded the previous day. This means bought and sold.

Example: In the case of Abbott Laboratories 3,100 shares were bought and 3,100 shares sold.

4. *Open. Open* refers to the price of the first hundred shares of stock that were traded. It may have occurred when the Exchange opened at 10 A.M. or at any time thereafter. The first 100 share lot of Abbott Laboratory was traded at 44½. There may have been more than 100 shares of stock traded at that price. This information can be obtained from special services or from the Stock Exchange.

High. This refers to the highest price of at least 100 shares traded that day. In the case of Abbott Laboratories it was at 45. As stated previously, more than 100 shares may have been traded.

Low. This refers to the lowest price at which at least 100 shares were traded. In the case of Abbott Laboratories it was $44.50.

Close. This is the last price at which at least 100 shares were traded. The last price may have been completed before noon. There are services which state the time of every trade.

5. *Net Change.* This refers to the price difference between the last trade this day by comparison with the previous day. In the case of Abbott Laboratories the stock closed the previous day at 44¾.

Where the stock sold x (meaning x-dividend) a more complex calculation has to be made. This will be done later, when dividends are considered. Looking down the list of names there are some, such as Air Prod. pf 4.75. This refers to a preferred stock that pays annual dividends of $4.75 a share. Sometimes, there are letters next to the dividend or volume. One should consult the index at the end of the list for their meaning.

Rights. From time to time corporations issue new stock or bonds by giving their stockholders the right to buy them at lower than the market price. These rights have a terminal date, and if not exercised by that time become worthless. Holiday Inn issued such rights in 1967. Note that 104,500 rights were traded the previous day.

Rights should be exercised or sold. Millions of dollars are lost each year by careless stockholders who forget to sell their rights or exercise them. If your stocks are held by brokers in street name you will be notified by them of this important asset.

Nov. 27, 1967

34⅜	19⅛	High Voltage	18[illegible]	24⅞	26	24½	25¼	
61⅜	15¼	HiltnHot 1.30	48	60⅞	62	59⅞	62	+1⅛
17¼	9½	Hoff Electrn	23	10⅛	10⅜	10⅛	10⅜	+ ⅛
[illegible]	[illegible]	Holida Inn rt	1045	½	9-16	15-32	9-16¾	1-16
55	38¾	HolidyInn .30	45	45¼	45¾	44¾	45¾	+ ½
39	17½	HollySug 1.20	83	31⅛	31¾	31⅛	31⅜	− ¼
54½	38½	Homestk .80b	497	54⅜	55¼	53½	54¾	+3¾
107⅜	63½	Honeywl 1.10	195	107	108	104⅛	107⅞	+ ⅞
118	82¼	Honeyw pf 3	10	118	118	117	117	−1
49½	34⅛	Hook Ch 1.40	36	36½	36½	36	36½	+ ¼
35½	22¼	Hoov Ball 1a	13	29½	30	29	30	+ ¼

Dividends. Most corporations pay dividends from their earnings at regular intervals. The Board of Directors meet and declare the dividends. The newspapers report this information in somewhat the following way.

In the first column is the name of the company; for example, Applebaums' Food Markets. (See page 139).

"Q" under period means that the dividend represents a quarterly payment of $.09 per share.

The dividend checks of Applebaums' Food Markets will be payable on January 2, 1968. That is the approximate date it should be received by the stockholders.

Nov. 27, 1967

Dividends Reported November 24-25

Company	Period	Amt.	Payable date	Record date
Applebaums' Food Mrkts	Q	.09	1 — 2 — 68	12 — 15
Bank of Delware	E	.25	12 — 13 — 67	12 — 4
Bank of Delware	Q	.40	12 — 13 — 67	12 — 4
Billups Western Petrol	Q	.12½	12 — 19 — 67	12 — 7
Camden Trust Co NJ	Q	.40	1 — 2 — 68	12 — 13
Canadian Marconi Co	S	.05	12 — 29 — 67	12 — 8
Central Penn Nat'l Bk	Q	.60	12 — 20 — 67	12 — 5
Central Penn Nat'l Bk ...	Sp	.25	12 — 20 — 67	12 — 5
Culligan Inc	Q	.12	12 — 22 — 67	12 — 8
Cunningham Drug Strs ...	°	.17½	12 — 20 — 67	12 — 5
Eaton & Howard Bal F°	h.14¾		12 — 20 — 67	12 — 1
Eaton & Howard B°'	50		12 — 20 — 67	12 — 1
Eaton & Howard			12 — 20 — 67	12 — 1
Eaton & Hov·			12 — 20 — 67	12 — 1
Fidelty B·			° — 30 — 67	12 — 15
First ᵀ			°5 — 68	12 — 29
Geʳ			67	12 — 1
ᶜ				12 — 5
			° — 15	
				·5

Who will get the dividend? Those stockholders whose names appear on the records of the corporation on December 15th will receive it. When stocks are bought or sold on the New York Stock Exchange, the broker notifies the bank that acts as the transfer agent for the company to delete the name of one stockholder and substitute another. This change takes approximately 4 business days. Counting back 4 business days from Friday, December 15, 1967, brings us to Monday, December 11, 1967. Those stockholders who buy or own the stock on Monday will be entitled to the dividend even if they sell it on the very next day. Those who buy the stock on Tuesday will not receive this dividend. The New York Stock Exchange has established the procedure that those who buy this stock on Tuesday, do so x-div., that is without the dividend. The seller receives the dividend.

Going back to page 136, last column on the right, "net change," those securities that sold x will show no change if they dropped by the amount of the dividend. Thus, if a stock sold at 45½ on Monday and was x-div 50¢ on Tuesday, there would be no change if it closed at 45 on Tuesday. If it closed above 45 on Tuesday the net change would be + the excess. On the other hand, if it closed below 45, the net change would be − the difference. If the dividend is 40c it is treated for the purpose of net dividend as ½ point.

Because of human error and technical difficulties, the change of ownership information does not always reach the corporation or its agent in sufficient time to delete the former stockholder and record the new one. Dividends may be sent to the former instead of the new one. In due time a letter is sent to the former stockholder advising him of the error and asking him to return the check that was not due him. The person who bought the security in time to receive the dividend misses it and makes his demand. Minor irritations occur. Those who buy a security before the x-div. date should be especially alert about receiving their first dividend.

There is an aspect involving the x-div. date that captures the imagination of some purchasers. They buy the security of their choice one or two days before the x-div. date to obtain the dividend. This practice is sufficiently widespread to move most securities upward prior to that time. The majority of securities close even or in the minus column on the x-div. date. Most people who buy a security a few days before the x-div. date are losers because they have to pay an income tax on the dividend. Our advice is not to buy a security to get that dividend. Wait until the x-div. date or a day or so thereafter. Normally, the price will be cheaper then. As for the seller, let the buyer get the dividend, especially if there is a long-term capital gain. Get the higher profit rather than the dividend. The income tax on long-term capital gains is less than on dividends.

Highs and Lows

Most morning newspapers list those securities that registered their highest prices of the year the previous day; also the lowest. An illustration appears on page 141.

There are some traders who watch the highs carefully. They have noted that most securities that make one high usually make a second, third, etc. This presents an opportunity for

Dec. 7, 1967

> # New 1967 Highs & Lows
> # On N.Y. Stock Exchange

Wednesday, December 6, 1967

NEW HIGHS-73

Alside Inc	Honeywell	Newmont pf
Am Photo	Honeywll pf	PerkElm wi
AvcoCp pf	HotelCp Am	Rayonier
Benguet	IntFlav Fra	Ryder Syst
Brunswk	Int Silver	StL San F pf
City Invest	IntT&T pf J	Sanders
Cluett Pea	ITE Ckt	Scient Data
Colt Indust	Jim Walter	Std Prud Un
Cook Coffee	Jim Walt pf	Stude Worth
Cooper TR	Jostens	Stu Wor pfB
Corning Gl	Kendall Co	StudeW pfA
Cruc Stl	Kresge SS	Swingline
DiaSham wi	Lanvin	Talon Inc
Domin Fund	LongILt pfI	TexGas Tra
Dow Chem	Macy RH	Textron
Eurofund	MacyRH ¦wi	Tish Real
Fafnir Bear	McDonald	TRW Inc
Fairmont	MAm Pipe	Twent Cent
Fairmont pf	Monog Ind	Unit EngFd
G Am Inves	Murphy Oil	Unit Util pf
Genesco Inc	MurO 4.90pf	Uris Bldg
GaPcf 1.40pf	Nt CashReg	VSI Corp
Green Shoe	Nat Svc Ind	Ward Foods
Gulton Ind	Nat Stand	
Hilton Hotel	Newmont	

NEW LOWS-52

AmInvest pf	ESB Inc	Pac T&T pf
Am Sug pf	Flintkt pf A	Ph El 3.80pf
Armour pf	Flintkt pf B	PhilM 3.90pf
Atchison	Gen Instr pf	PSEG 5.28pf
Bran Airw	HuntFd pfA	PSEG 4.30pf
Carrier pf	HuntFd pfB	PSEG 1.40pf
Celan 7 pf	IllPw 4.08pf	Seab Fin pf
Celan pf A	Interst Pw	Std Brand
Cen Hud Gl	Iowa PL	StdBrand pf
Clev Pit spl	Jones L pf	Sunasco
ColgPalm pf	Ligg My pf	Sunasco pf
Coml Cr pf	Lorillard pf	Union Elec
Comw Edis	NewEng TT	Va EP 5 pf
Delta Air	NiagM Pow	Wn Air Lin
Duq 4.20 pf	NoNG 5.80pf	WnUn 4.60pf
Duq 4.10 pf	Nwst Airlin	Wheel Stl
Duq Lt 4 pf	OhEd 4.56pf	
East Util As	Pac Sw Airl	

quick profits. This aspect was researched and the late Burton Crane published the results in a special article in the Sunday *New York Times* several years ago. It was found that there are a few securities that make as many as twenty. However, one cannot predict which securities will do what. Although there may be some skillful traders who can take advantage of this fact, most individuals abandon this experiment after several losses.

The experience with the lows is similar. If a security makes a low for the year it will probably make another. Here too, there is a spectrum, from those that make only one to a few that make many. The thesis in this book is to watch those that make their first low. They should be charted and studied as suggested in the early chapters of this book and purchased when the pattern suggests a reversal of trend. By and large, with very few exceptions, both the good-quality as well as those that are not so good reverse their trend at some time and move upward, as described in Chapter 1.

The highs and lows often present other important information. For example, they indicate which groups are most desired and which are under selling pressure. Where a group is popular it should be studied *for the laggards.* For some unknown reason there may be one or two securities that remain behind the group, only to be discovered later. Investors who do so first often turn their information to profits. One should not buy a laggard mechanically. It may be a case of poor earnings. On the other hand it may be purely accidental. Research should give the answer.

Where a group is under selling pressure it should be studied for the best time to buy. There is no need to rush because there is little likelihood of a sudden turnabout. Months may elapse. In fact, it may be best to wait until the tax-selling period of November and December.

Oct. 23, 1967

MOST ACTIVE STOCKS

	Open	High	Low	Close	Chg.	Volume
Pan Am Sul	40⅜	41¼	39½	39¾	....	214,000
Fairch Cam	83	83	79½	80⅞	−5	169,800
Ford Mot	52⅞	52⅞	52	52¼	− ¾	118,900
Allis Chalm	38⅛	38⅝	37½	38¼	+ ¼	115,400
Thiokol	20½	20⅞	20	20⅛	− ½	115,200
Wolve W W	18⅞	19	17¼	18	−1	100,900
Am Tel Tel	51¼	51⅜	51	51	− ¼	99,400
Pittston Co	56⅛	59	55¾	58⅝	+2¾	86,400
Univ Amer	24¼	25	24⅛	25	+ ¾	85,300
Webb Del E	7½	7½	6⅝	6⅞	− ⅝	82,100

Most Active List

Some traders make much of this information and even trade by it. It is of limited importance. Where a stock has been under long selling pressure, extremely heavy volume sometimes signals the end of the selling, especially where the large volume failed to depress the security. On the other hand, unusually large volume when the stock is moving up may signal the end of the move, for the time being. It may even be the end of the move for the year. Repeating the point made previously, technical aspects other than volume are more important.

Bonds

Here is a sample of bond prices.

Oct. 23, 1967

Corporation Bonds
Volume, $15,350,000

A-B-C-D

--1967--			Sales in				Net
High	Low	Bonds	$1,000	High	Low	Close	Chg.
140¼	105	Air Red cv3⅞s87	68	114½	111	111	−3⅝
152½	110	Allegh L cv4s81	11	135	133½	135	+1⅞
86½	82	Allied Ch 3⅛s78	15	81⅝	81⅝	81⅝	− ⅜
146	92½	Allied St cv4¼-ᵒ⸁	30	134	134	134	−1
98⅞	96½	Allied Str ⸀	170	97½	96¼	96¼	−2¼
101	99½	Alcoa ⸀	⸀	99¼	99	99¼	..
130¾	111¾	Aⅰ⸀	⸀5	113¾	114¼	− ¾
94	82				82¼	82¼	− ⅜
104	⸀					103	−1
¹⁷ᵖ⸀					¹¹		−2
							− ½

Government Issues

Here is a list of Treasury Bills and Bonds.

Oct. 23, 1967

U.S. Treas. Bills						U.S. Treas. Notes			
Mat	Bid	Ask	Mat	Bid	Ask	Rate	Mat	Bid	Asked	Yld
	Discount			Discount						
10-26	4.10	3.80	2-23	4.82	4.72	4⅞	11-67	100.1	100.3	3.23
10-31	4.10	3.80	2-29	4.85	4.76	5⅝	2-68	100.6	100.8	4.76
11- 2	4.15	3.90	3- 7	4.86	4.78	1½	4-68	98.16	98.22	4.56
11- 9	4.15	4.95	3-14	4.87	4.79	4¾	5-68	99.23	99.25	5.15
11-16	4.15	3.95	3- 2	4.92	4.84	4¼	8-68	99.4	99.6	5.29
11-24	4.19	4.05	3-22	4.89	4.86	1½	10-68	97.6	97.10	4.46
11-30	4.21	4.09	3-28	4.96	4.90	5¼	11-68	99.26	99.28	5 37
12- 1	4.20	4.10	3-31	4.94	4.85	1½	4-69	95.10	95.18	4.73
12-14	4.14	4.04	4- 4	5.03	4.98	1½	10-69	93.28	94.4	4.71
12-21	4.16	4.06	4-11	5.08	4.04	1½	4-70	92.14	92.18	4.77
12-28	4.18	4.10	4-18	5.09	5.06	1½	10-70	91.2	91.18	4.60
12-31	4.23	4.12	4-22	5.10	5.07	5	11-70	98.18	98.22	5.47
1- 4	4.48	4.41	4-30	5.12	5.03	5⅝	2-71	99.18	99.20	5.50
1-11	4.56	4.51	5-31	5.16	5.09	1½	4-71	89.18	89.28	4.73
1-18	4.58	4.55	5-24	5.26	5.23	5¼	5-71	99.9	99.13	5.44
1-25	4.62	4.53	5-30	5.26	5.22	1½	10-71	88.8	88.24	4.66
1-31	4.64	4.54	1-31	5.23	5.13	5⅜	11-71	99.18	99.21	5.47
						4¾	2-72	96.27	96.31	5.55

The list of government bonds is printed in many newspapers.

Over-the-Counter

There are literally thousands of securities that are traded "over-the-counter," in fact many more than in the listed markets. Here is a small sample.

Dec. 7, 1967

Over-the-Counter Markets

A							
Stock & Div.	Bid	Asked	Bid Chg.	Stock & Div.	Bid	Asked	Bid Chg.
				CrdthrftF 1.30	22¼	23	.....
				Crescent Tech	7¾	8¼	.....
A A I Corp	23	25	.....	Cromptn 1.40a	32½	33¾	− ¼
Acme Elec .16	20½	21½	.....	CrossComp .40	39¼	40¼	− ¼
Acme ndusts	6½	7	....	Culligan In .48	49½	51	+ 2½
Acme Vis .30b	58	59	+ ¾	Cyber Tronics	11½	12	+ ¾
Acushnet .50g	26½	27½	.....	**D**			
Adley Corp	5⅞	6⅜	....				
Advance Ross	15¼	15¾	− ½	DallasArm .50	33	34	− ½
Affil Hosp Pd	22½	23½	+ 1½	Danly Mach 1	19¼	19¾	− ⅛
Air California	18½	18⅝	+ ⅜	Dasa Corperat	14½	15	− ⅞
Airborn Frght	9¼	9¾	....	Data Products	22¾	23⅛	− ½
Airlift Internl	6¼	6½	− ⅛	DaytonCp .20b	53	54	− ½
Ala TenNG .80	13⅝	14⅛	....	DaytonMal .80	34⅝	35½	+ ¼
Albertsons .36	10½	10⅞	− ⅛	D C Inter .60	17½	18	.....
AlcoStand .10b	39¼	40¼	+ 1¾	Dean Foods 1	20	21	.....
Alcon Lab .40	49	50	.....	De.. Ltd	8⅜	8⅝	− ⅛
Alico Land Dv	9⅞	10¼	...	.il	2⅜	2⅝	....
AllegPepsi .40	13¾	137..			36¼	37¾	+ ½
Allied Equit	16¾	1..		..⅛	10⅝	...	
Allied Radio	15..					17¼	− ¼
Allied Thr 1½						.8¼	.....
Allyn Bacn							+ ½
AloeCre..							
Alp..							..,

Your broker has a complete list of over-the-counter securities, printed on "Pink" sheets. These should be consulted if any significant trading is done in this area. Do not buy a security without paying a commission. It may be more expensive. Use your broker as your buying or selling agent. If you buy without paying a commission you will have little recourse if you overpay. You are buying from a principal.

Tax-Exempts

Some newspapers publish a very small sampling of municipal and state bonds. Your broker receives a Blue Book daily which contains thousands of tax-exempts from every community and state. If you want to buy a tax-exempt have your broker check the Blue Book and make recommendations from it. Long-term tax-exempts should not be bought, because of inflation. If and when the Vietnam war ends and the inflation subsides these securities may once more be worth considering.

Summary of Chapter

In this chapter a few technical matters to reduce friction between client and broker have been considered as well as the highlights of reading a newspaper. Those who want more detailed information should consult pamphlets issued by the New York Stock Exchange and other exchanges and books on how to read the financial pages of a newspaper. Many technical aspects of trading have been deliberately avoided which affect only a few highly sophisticated individuals and professionals. If the average investor gets too engrossed in these he may ignore the fundamental aspects.

8
Funds

More and more people are relying on funds to do their investing for them. The industry has grown from humble origins to one that is nearing the $40 billion mark.

Kinds of Funds

There are two kinds of funds: the open-end and the closed-end.

Closed-End Funds

A closed-end fund is a fund, organized as a corporation, with a fixed number of shares outstanding. The number may be increased by year-end stock dividends and the occasional sale of additional shares of stock. By and large, the number of shares is relatively limited. A list of closed-end funds with net asset value is reported weekly in the *Wall Street Journal* and other newspapers. (See page 148).

The stock of a closed-end fund can be purchased from a person who already owns it and who wishes to sell his shares. This is the same as for any other listed or unlisted stock. The stock of a closed-end fund cannot be purchased from the fund itself or sold back to it. This is the most important difference between the open- and the closed-end funds.

The auction market determines the price at which these funds are traded, regardless of their intrinsic value. A fund may

Closed-End Funds

Friday, November 24, 1967
Following is a weekly listing of unaudited net asset
values of closed-end investment fund shares, reported by
the companies as of Friday's close. Also shown is the
closing listed market price or a dealer-to-dealer asked
price of each fund's shares, with the percentage of difference.

Dec. 27, 1967

	N.A. Value	Stk Price	% Diff		N.A. Value	Stk Price	% Diff
Abacus	18.18	16	−12.0	Madison	23.79	27⅝	+ 21 2
AdmExp	34.07	31⅞	− 6.4	NatlAvia	38.29	48	+2˜ 4
AmEuro	44.05	35	−20.5	NiagraSh	24 90	22⅞	− 8 1
AmIntl	19.25	17½	− 9.1	OseasSec	10.83	22¼	+ 10
Carriers	36.44	29¼	−19.7	PetroCp	22.71	23	+ ' ˜
Dominick	31.12	26¾	−17.3	StdSh(a)	27.39	22⅞	−16.5
GenInv	39.29	36¼	− 7.7	Tri-Contl	36.35	28	˜23 0
GenPubS	7.61	6¾	−11.3	United	12.62	11¾	− 9.8
IntlHold	20.69	17¼	−16.6	US&For	42.10	35	−1˜.˜
Japan	14.92	14½	− 2.8	Ex-dividend.			
Lehman	20.59	20⅝	− 1.1				

be worth $30 per share, based on the value of its holdings. However, if no one wants to pay that much for the stock it may have to sell for as little as $25. By way of example, not so many years ago the stock of the Lehman Corporation sold at a premium of 15% above the value of their underlying holdings. During 1956 and 1957 it sold at discounts as large as 15%.

Going back to the list of closed-end funds shown above, note the different discounts at which most of them were selling as of the date indicated. One should not assume that the larger the discount, the poorer the fund. It only means that at this time there is little demand for it. A study of the discounts and premiums at which they sell shows neither logic nor pattern. Those who want to buy a closed-end fund should examine its financial statement, study its portfolio and its past record. If they are satisfactory, that fund should be purchased which is selling at the greatest discount.

Open-End Funds (Also Called Mutual Funds)

An open-end fund is one that has no fixed number of shares that may be outstanding. At one time it may be 100,000. The very next day it may increase or decrease depending on new purchases or redemptions. If many individuals want to purchase the stock of a fund, it simply issues new shares. If people want their shares redeemed, it reduces the number outstanding.

The stock of an open-end fund must be bought directly from the fund or its authorized agent. And, as has been stated, if a holder wishes to sell his shares, he must sell them to the fund itself.

The price paid for the stock is based on the net asset value, plus a "loading" charge, if any. When redeemed, the amount one receives is likewise based on the net asset value, minus a sales fee, if any. In short, the value of the stock of an open-end fund is based on the net asset value, plus or minus certain charges, if any, and not on an auction market. As stated previously, this is an important difference between open-end and closed-end funds.

Although the number of closed-end funds is small, the number of open-end ones is large and growing. Here is a partial list of the larger ones.

Mutual Funds

Friday, November 17, 1967

Price ranges for investment companies, as supplied by the National Association of Securities Dealers:

Nov. 20, 1967

	Bid	Asked	Chg		Bid	Asked	Chg
Aberdeen	3.13	3.42	(z)	Johnst (v)	21.69	21.69+	.16
Adviser F'd	8.64	9.49+	.10	Keystone Custodian Funds:			
Affiliated	8.30	8.98+	.03	Invst B 1	21.30	22.23	....
All Am F'd	1.23	1.34	....	MedGB 2	22.69	24.75+	.02
Am Bus Sh	3.71	4.01+	.01	Disct B 4	9.80	10.70−	.01
AmDiv Inv	11.55	12.62+	.04	Incm K 1	8.99	9.82+	.05
Am Grwth	7.40	8.04	....	Grth K 2	7.77	8.48+	.07
AmInv (v)⁄	38.10	38.10+	.57	HihGrS 1	22.03	24.04+	.15
Am Mutual	10.08	11.02+	.02	Incm S 2	10.71	11.69+	.08
Am Pacific	(z)	(z)	(z)	GrwthS 3	9.62	10.50+	.10
Assoc Fnd	1.59	1.74	....	LowP S 4	6.98	7.62+	.20
As Inv (v)	x7.58	7.58−	.05	Keystn Intl	15.44	16.70+	.32
Axe-Houghton:				K‾ ‾ᵈ	7.15	7.84+	.01
Fund A	7.69	8.36+	‾ ‾		12.84	14.06+	.03
Fund B	10.15	1¹ ʹ			ⁿᵒ	10.93+	.03
Stock F'd	7 ʳ‾				ʹ⁹	.16+	.12
Axe Sci⁻					‾ ᶫ	.01	
Blu⁻ ‾							ⁿ²

Loading Charge

The "loading" charge is an initiation fee that some funds charge. Most of it represents salesmen's commissions and selling expenses.

In the case of the first fund in the list, Aberdeen, the loading charge is 9%. This is obtained by noting that the *asked* price is 9% more than the *bid*. It is 9.8% for the Advisers Fund. There is no loading charge for the Assc Inv., because the *bid* and *asked* prices are the same.

One should not assume that a loading charge is in any way associated with the fund's performance. They are in no way related. Performance is the result of investment policy.

One may wonder how the no-load funds pay their expenses. All funds, open-end and closed-end, load and no-load, have expenses. These are taken from the fund's income. This has nothing to do with the loading charge, which is strictly part of selling expenses.

Fund Policy

Each fund has its own policy or objective. There is the "balanced" fund which invests part of its funds in bonds and the rest in common stock. Then there are all kinds of "growth" funds that invest most of their money in common stocks. Some limit themselves to "standard" securities which are purchased when they are depressed. Others seek the more "bizarre" variety. There are funds that purchase securities in only one industry such as oils, utilities or airlines. Most funds diversify.

A new kind of fund has just appeared on the scene. It is called the dual purpose fund. It is divided into two parts, for those who want dividends only and for those who want capital gains only. This is no doubt intended to satisfy those who want income and those who want capital gains.

There are two ways of determining the objectives or policy of the fund. One way is to read its prospectus. This is a statement which describes its objectives and furnishes other information about the fund. By far the better way is to examine its operating portfolio. Funds issue their statements regularly. Look at the list. Does it contain the kind of securities you would want to own and is its record satisfactory? This defines its policy better than the language in the prospectus.

Diversification

One of the virtues of a fund is its diversification. Unlike the average investor, who must limit himself to a few stocks, the fund with its vast resources can purchase securities from many industries. On page 152 is a summary of the diversified policy of one of the closed-end funds, the Lehman Corporation.

Comparison of funds is no easy matter. The arithmetic is simple enough. All that one has to do is to start the comparison on a certain date, note the value of the funds on that day and the value on a later comparison date. Adjustments are then made for distributions of dividends and capital gains. However, the problem is more complicated.

Consider a fund that started several years ago and which concentrated on utilities, when they were in demand. It would have done brilliantly for several years. On a short-term basis, it would have outperformed the oils during their poorer period. Or consider a fund that specialized in insurance securities, when they outperformed even the finest growth stocks. They too did remarkably well for several years. Thus, the investor could move from one glamour group to another and to the funds that invested heavily in them. They shone like meteors, only to fade. In short, comparing funds over a short period of time is fraught with danger.

It is advisable to select a fund which has a widely diversified portfolio and a satisfactory record. Common stock funds are favored for protection against inflation. Obtain a list of the securities held and study the portfolio. Does it include the major economic areas? If it does, then examine its performance record for the past decade. Has it done satisfactorily? Use the following steps to determine its performance:

Step 1. Value of fund at present time
   2. Value of fund ten years ago
   3. Increase in value
   4. Add distribution of dividends and capital gains
   5. Add step 3 and 4 to obtain total increase
   6. Divide step 5 by step 2 to obtain percent increase
   7. Using a compound interest table determine the annual yield

THE LEHMAN CORPORATION

	Cost per Books	Value	Percentage of Net Assets
Cash, U.S. Government Obligations and Receivables (less current liabilities)	$ 8,328,492	$ 8,328,304	1.7%
Corporate Obligations	$ 1,713,014	$ 1,907,875	.4%
Preferred Stocks	$ 8,126,691	$ 10,963,000	2.3%
Common Stocks:			
Chemical	$ 12,647,854	$ 33,895,560	6.9%
Drug & Cosmetic	13,345,963	60,413,750	12.4
Education & Recreation	3,942,896	6,847,850	1.4
Electronics & Electrical Equipment	13,589,803	34,667,674	7.1
Food & Beverage	8,707,128	22,209,375	4.5
Forest Products	4,724,547	9,085,675	1.9
Insurance	8,330,911	8,562,500	1.8
Machinery & Equipment	6,830,782	9,912,988	2.0
Manufacturing & Miscellaneous	17,433,316	34,873,784	7.1
Merchandising	5,332,379	20,693,500	4.2
Metal & Mining	7,321,170	22,968,750	4.7
Office Equipment	9,012,863	92,297,600	18.9
Oil & Gas	10,771,730	55,898,227	11.4
Packaging	4,560,534	8,220,716	1.7
Public Utility	23,088,413	43,850,107	9.0
Other Common Stocks	1,951,656	2,185,900	.4
	$151,591,945	$466,583,956	95.4%
Miscellaneous Investments	$ 92,709	$ 1,165,000	.2%
Net Assets before an allowance for taxes on unrealized appreciation	$169,852,851	$488,948,135	100.0%
Allowance for State and City taxes on unrealized appreciation [see note (1) page 25]		1,760,000	
Net Asset Value		$487,188,135	

Example:

The facts:

Value of Fund 10 years ago	$10.00 a share
Value of Fund today	15.00 a share
Dividends and Capital Gains distributed	5.15 a share

Calculation:

Step 1.	Value of fund today	$15.00 a share
2.	Value of fund ten years ago	10.00 a share
3.	Increase in value	5.00 a share
4.	Add distributions of dividends and capital gains	5.15 a share
5.	Total increase	10.15 a share
6.	Divide amount in Step 5 by amount in Step 2 and get 101.5%	

Consulting a compound interest table, this represents a yield of slightly less than 8% annually (before taxation). If $1 is invested at 8% for ten years, compounded annually, it will increase by 115%.

This method of calculation is only approximate. The dividend and capital gain distributions made during the ten years were not compounded. If this were done, the yield would have been higher than the 101.5%. Despite this, the method represents a workable approximation.

Contractual Plans

Whether one invests in an open-end fund with or without a load charge or in a closed-end fund is a matter of personal preference. Those who want greater reward and are willing to take the proportionate risk should consider the more speculative funds. However, we do not recommend the "front-end" contractual plans. Here, the buyer contracts to deposit a fixed monthly sum for a given period of time. Our objection is only to the substantial loading charge, which amounts to almost 50% of the first year's deposits. We have

seen contractual plans in existence for 5 years where, at the end
of this period, the investor's holdings were less than his deposits
though he reinvested all his dividends and capital gains. This is
indeed a savings program at an exorbitant cost.

Unfortunately many individuals who sign for contractual
plans are not aware of the heavy charges during the first year.
They are dazzled by picturesque long-range charts which do not
apply to those who enter these plans.

The S.E.C. Report

The Securities and Exchange Commission has made an
exhaustive study of funds and has come forth with many
suggestions for change. They oppose the "front end" loads
because of the heavy charges.

They also object to the fees charged by those who manage
these funds, considering many of them excessive. However, they
have shied away from evaluating performance.

Recommendations

Funds serve a valuable function because they have
continuous management. They meet the needs of most
individuals, from those who prefer speculative issues to those
who seek conservative ones. They are especially suited for trusts
and estates. Self-employed persons may invest in them if they
join the Keogh Plan. They can be used by people of modest
means to "dollar" average. This means that the investor can
deposit a fixed amount of money at regular intervals. In a rising
market, he buys fewer shares and in a poor market, more shares.
This results in a better overall performance than could be
obtained by buying the same number of shares regularly.

The approach in this book has been a relatively conservative
one. The objective has been to earn a steady stream of profits
each and every year, rather than making a spectacular gain in
one year. A fund whose investments contain standard securities,
and whose long-term record has been good is better. This meets
the criterion of protection against inflation.

9
The Economy

A detailed study of the American economy can be the work of a lifetime. However, there are a few highlights with which the investor should be familiar so that he can evaluate economic events calmly and correctly. Each year has its dramatic moments. A President is shot. A war breaks out between the Arab states and Israel. To curb inflation, the Administration and the Federal Reserve Bank tighten money and make it scarce. What are the probable consequences? Should one panic, sell his holdings and wait for normalcy to return? A successful investor should be able to face these and other serious problems and appraise them or, at least, seek an answer.

Although some individuals act as though investments were akin to horse racing, the fact is that they are an essential and integral part of the economy. A depression plays havoc with people's fortunes. A healthy, expanding economy acts as a guardian of savings and property.

Before looking at salient aspects of our own economy, take note of the sources of information that are available.

Most important are the newspapers. Each day's national and local events, when synthesized, present a picture of the nation. Then, there are numerous magazines, some of a general nature, others specifically limited to business and investments. For information about a specific corporation, annual reports can be obtained by writing to the company. Summaries are published by the Standard & Poor Corporation. Brokerage houses usually contain a complete file of financial reports. The different exchanges publish pamphlets which are available on request. There are numerous U.S. Government publications which contain detailed economic information. A list can be obtained from the Superintendent of Documents, U.S. Government Printing Office, Washington, D.C. 20402. Specifically, we should like to mention three basic publications:

Survey of Current Business—cost $6.00 per year for domestic and $9.75 for foreign mailing. This is published monthly with weekly supplements.

The Economic Report of the President—cost $1.25

Statistical Abstract of the United States—cost $3.75

There are literally hundreds of specialized "tip" sheets, purporting to "guide you to that fortune." Some are worthy; others worthless. Some employ the latest electronic devices in their prognostications. These are no better than the individuals who prepare them. An electronic machine only correlates the information that is fed into it. If the programming is faultily designed, the result will suffer accordingly. Our opinion is, that except for a few of the more complete services, which give information and analysis rather than "hot" tips, the investor would do better to save his money.

Our Strong Economy

No one will dispute the fact that the American economy is the strongest in the world. This is no accidental matter but the result of many factors, of which the following are significant:

1. Raw materials in sufficient quantity to satisfy the economic needs of its population.

2. A scientific community, well educated, to create and improve necessary machinery and equipment.

3. A managerial group that can organize and maintain production efficiently.

4. A skilled work force.

5. An adequate transportation system.

6. A capitalist class that is willing to invest its surplus funds in the economy rather than in foreign nations.

7. A currency system that smooths the flow of goods and services.

8. A public sufficiently affluent to be able to purchase the goods that can be produced.

9. A stable government that guards against excesses, is alert to deficiencies that need correction and yet does not interfere with the normal functioning of business.

10. A system of taxation that discourages the accumulation of wealth in the hands of a few families. At the same time, it does not impoverish the people so that they cannot purchase the goods that are produced.

Our economy will be healthy only as long as these supports remain strong. Should poor judgment and errors weaken them, deterioration will set in as has happened in other great empires.

With this brief introduction, we should like to examine, at this point, an aspect of the economy that is particularly important to investors.

The Gross National Product

The Gross National Product reflects the expenditures of the most important areas of the national economy: personal consumption; gross private domestic investment; net exports of goods and services; and government purchases of goods and services.

The following table summarizes these expenditures from 1929 to 1966.

The most important factor revealed in the table is the continuous growth of the economy. Despite lapses here and there, the overall pattern has been one of continuous expansion. In 1929, for example, the GNP stood at $103.1 billion. Despite the severe depression of 1929-32, it rose to $785 billion by 1967, an increase of 660%. Even if we adjust the figures for the inflation, the increase is 230%.

NATIONAL INCOME OR EXPENDITURE

Table B-1.—Gross national product or expenditure, 1929-67
(Billions of dollars)

Year or quarter	Total gross national product	Personal consumption expenditures[1]	Gross private domestic investment[2]	Net exports of goods and services[3]	Government purchases of goods and services				
					Total	Federal[4]			State and local
						Total	National defense[5]	Other	
1929	103.1	77.2	16.2	1.1	8.5	1.3	1.3		7.2
1930	90.4	69.9	10.3	1.0	9.2	1.4	1.4		7.8
1931	75.8	60.5	5.6	.5	9.2	1.5	1.5		7.7
1932	58.0	48.6	1.0	.4	8.1	1.5	1.5		6.6
1933	55.6	45.8	1.4	.4	8.0	2.0	2.0		6.0
1934	65.1	51.3	3.3	.6	9.8	3.0	3.0		6.8
1935	72.2	55.7	6.4	.1	10.0	2.9	2.9		7.1
1936	82.5	61.9	8.5	.1	12.0	4.9	4.9		7.0
1937	90.4	66.5	11.8	.3	11.9	4.7	4.7		7.2
1938	84.7	63.9	6.5	.3	13.0	5.4	5.4		7.6
1939	90.5	66.8	9.3	1.3	13.3	5.1	1.2	3.9	8.2
1940	99.7	70.8	13.1	1.1	14.0	6.0	2.2	3.8	8.0
1941	124.5	80.6	17.9	1.7	24.8	16.9	13.8	3.1	7.9
1942	157.9	88.5	9.8	1.3	59.6	51.9	49.4	2.5	7.7

Year									
1943	191.6	99.3	5.7	−2.0	88.6	81.1	79.7	1.4	7.4
1944	210.1	108.3	7.1	−1.8	96.5	89.0	87.4	1.6	7.5
1945	211.9	119.7	10.6	−.6	82.3	74.2	73.5	.7	8.1
1946	208.5	143.4	30.6	7.5	27.0	17.2	14.7	2.5	9.8
1947	231.3	160.7	34.0	11.5	25.1	12.5	9.1	3.5	12.6
1948	257.6	173.6	46.0	6.4	31.6	16.5	10.7	5.8	15.0
1949	256.5	176.8	35.7	6.1	37.8	20.1	13.3	6.8	17.7
1950	284.8	191.0	54.1	1.8	37.9	18.4	14.1	4.3	19.5
1951	328.4	206.3	59.3	3.7	59.1	37.7	33.6	4.1	21.5
1952	345.5	216.7	51.9	2.2	74.7	51.8	45.9	5.9	22.9
1953	364.6	230.0	52.6	.4	81.6	57.0	48.7	8.4	24.6
1954	364.8	236.5	51.7	1.8	74.8	47.4	41.2	6.2	27.4
1955	398.0	254.4	67.4	2.0	74.2	44.1	38.6	5.5	30.1
1956	419.2	266.7	70.0	4.0	78.6	45.6	40.3	5.3	33.0
1957	441.1	281.4	67.8	5.7	86.1	49.5	44.2	5.3	36.6
1958	447.3	290.1	60.9	2.2	94.2	53.6	45.9	7.7	40.6
1959	483.7	311.2	75.3	.1	97.0	53.7	46.0	7.6	43.3
1960	503.7	325.2	74.8	4.0	99.6	53.5	44.9	8.6	46.1
1961	520.1	335.2	71.7	5.6	107.6	57.4	47.8	9.6	50.2
1962	560.3	355.1	83.0	5.1	117.1	63.4	51.6	11.8	53.7
1963	590.5	375.0	87.1	5.9	122.5	64.2	50.8	13.5	58.2
1964	632.4	401.2	94.0	8.5	128.7	65.2	50.0	15.2	63.5
1965	683.9	433.1	107.4	6.9	136.4	66.8	50.1	16.7	69.6
1966	743.3	465.9	118.0	5.1	154.3	77.0	60.5	16.5	77.2
1967p	785.1	491.6	112.1	5.0	176.3	89.9	72.6	17.3	86.4

(From *Economic Report of the President of the United States*, January 1967, page 209)

Growth is particularly important to the investor, because this is the climate in which the corporate enterprises in which he invests flourish. The steel, oil, rubber and chemical companies, to mention only a few, expanded with the economy. Those individuals who purchased good-quality securities many years ago are well aware of this fact. Despite the perennial fluctuations, the value of their holdings has increased substantially.

Growth of an economy is important for a second reason: It provides an area for the investment of savings. What happens to the savings of individuals and business organizations? In 1967, for example, they amounted to $112 billion. This is the amount that remained after all expenditures and the payment of taxes. These savings found their way back into the economy through the channel of gross private domestic investment or as loans to the Federal or local governments.

Refer to the third column of the GNP chart and note the increasing expenditures for private investment. It amounted to 14.3% of the GNP for 1967.

The relationship between savings and investments can be seen in the table on facing page covering almost four decades from 1929 to 1967.

This table presents succinctly the relationship between savings and their disposition. During normal years, such as 1960, most of the savings reverted to the economy by investments in industrial expansion. A small part was loaned to government. During war years, such as during the 1940's, most of it went as loans to the government, whose expenditures resulted in huge deficits.

The savings of individuals and business organizations contain the seeds for industrial expansion.

Can Growth Go On Forever?

This philosophical question, though not related to the immediate problem of investors, is important for the longer

Table B-18.—Sources and uses of gross saving, 1929-67
(Billions of dollars)

Year or quarter	Gross private saving and government surplus or deficit, national income and product accounts								Gross investment			
	Total	Private saving			Government surplus or deficit (−)				Total	Gross private domestic investment	Net foreign investment[1]	Statistical discrepancy
		Total	Personal saving	Gross business saving	Total	Federal	State and local					
1929	16.3	15.3	4.2	11.2	1.0	1.2	−0.2	17.0	16.2	0.8	0.7
1930	11.8	12.1	3.4	8.6	−.3	.3	−.6	11.0	10.3	.7	−.8
1931	5.1	8.0	2.6	5.3	−2.9	−2.1	−.8	5.8	5.6	.2	.7
1932	.8	2.5	−.6	3.2	−1.8	−1.5	−.3	1.1	1.0	.2	.3
1933	.9	2.3	−.9	3.2	−1.4	−1.3	−.1	1.6	1.4	.2	.6
1934	3.2	5.6	.4	5.2	−2.4	−2.9	.5	3.8	3.3	.4	.5
1935	6.6	8.6	2.1	6.4	−2.0	−2.6	.6	6.4	6.4	−.1	−.2
1936	7.2	10.3	3.6	6.7	−3.1	−3.6	.5	8.4	8.5	−.1	1.2
1937	11.9	11.5	3.8	7.7	.3	−.4	.7	11.8	11.8	.1	#
1938	7.0	8.7	.7	8.0	−1.8	−2.1	.4	7.6	6.5	1.1	.6
1939	8.8	11.0	2.6	8.4	−2.2	−2.2	(2)	10.2	9.3	.9	1.3
1940	13.6	14.3	3.8	10.5	−.7	−1.3	.6	14.6	13.1	1.5	1.0
1941	18.6	22.4	11.0	11.4	−3.8	−5.1	1.3	19.0	17.9	1.1	.4

Year											
1942	10.7	42.0	27.6	14.5	−31.4	−33.1	1.8	9.6	9.8	−.2	−1.1
1943	5.5	49.7	33.4	16.3	−44.1	−46.6	2.5	3.5	5.7	−2.2	−2.0
1944	2.5	54.3	37.3	17.1	−51.8	−54.5	2.7	5.0	7.1	−2.1	2.5
1945	5.2	44.7	29.6	15.1	−39.5	−42.1	2.6	9.1	10.6	−1.4	3.9
1946	35.1	29.7	15.2	14.5	5.4	3.5	1.9	35.2	30.6	4.6	.1
1947	42.0	27.5	7.3	20.2	14.4	13.4	1.0	42.9	34.0	8.9	.9
1948	49.9	41.4	13.4	28.0	8.5	8.4	.1	47.9	46.0	1.9	−2.0
1949	35.9	39.0	9.4	29.7	−3.2	−2.4	−.7	36.2	35.7	.5	.3
1950	50.4	42.5	13.1	29.4	7.8	9.1	−1.2	51.8	54.1	−2.2	1.5
1951	56.1	50.3	17.3	33.1	5.8	6.2	−.4	59.5	59.3	.2	3.3
1952	49.5	53.3	18.1	35.1	−3.8	−3.8	(3)	51.6	51.9	−.3	2.2
1953	47.5	54.4	18.3	36.1	−6.9	−7.0	.1	50.5	52.6	−2.1	3.0
1954	48.5	55.6	16.4	39.2	−7.0	−5.9	−1.1	51.3	51.7	−.5	2.7
1955	64.8	62.1	15.8	46.3	2.7	4.0	−1.3	66.9	67.4	−.5	2.1
1956	72.7	67.8	20.6	47.3	4.9	5.7	−.9	71.6	70.0	1.5	−1.1
1957	71.2	70.5	20.7	49.8	.7	2.1	−1.4	71.2	67.8	3.4	*
1958	59.2	71.7	22.3	49.4	−12.5	−10.2	−2.3	60.7	60.9	−.2	1.6
1959	73.8	75.9	19.1	56.8	−2.1	−1.2	−.8	73.0	75.3	−2.3	−.8
1960	77.5	73.9	17.0	56.8	3.7	3.5	.2	76.5	74.8	1.7	−1.0
1961	75.5	79.8	21.2	58.7	−4.3	−3.8	−.5	74.7	71.7	3.0	−.8
1962	85.0	87.9	21.6	66.3	−2.9	−3.8	.9	85.5	83.0	2.5	.5
1963	90.5	88.7	19.9	68.8	1.8	.7	1.2	90.3	87.1	3.1	−.3
1964	101.0	102.4	26.2	76.2	−1.4	−3.0	1.7	99.7	94.0	5.7	−1.3
1965	113.5	110.8	27.2	83.7	2.7	1.4	1.2	111.5	107.4	4.1	−2.0
1966	122.7	119.5	29.8	89.7	3.2	.3	2.9	120.2	118.0	2.2	−2.6
1967p	116.5	129.2	38.7	90.4	−12.7	−12.6	−.1	114.1	112.1	2.0	−2.2

view. Nothing expands forever. History has demonstrated this. Raw materials, though substantial, are not without limit. Water supply and fresh air, though plentiful, become inadequate, polluted and a destructive factor. The recent power failures serve as a warning. The fact of the matter is that we should not take our economy for granted. It needs a lot of watching for weak spots, which should be anticipated and corrected. Within the normal limitations of land, fresh air, pure water, sunshine, the intelligent utilization of our natural resources and conservation, our continued growth can be assured for a long time.

Depressions and Recessions

Implicit in the operation of our economy is the delicate balance between production and consumption. Factories and farms produce an abundance of goods and these must be purchased by organizations and individuals within a reasonable period of time. When a dislocation occurs between the capacity to produce and the ability to consume, a recession (which is short and slight) or a depression (which is serious and long) develops. Going back to the Table B-1 (page 158), the years 1930 through 1933 reflect a period of severe depression. Personal consumption expenditures dropped from $77.2 billion in 1929 to $45.8 billion for 1933, a decrease of 39%. Gross private domestic investment fell from $16.2 billion in 1929 to $1.4 billion, a decrease of more than 91%. Government spending stood still.

Subsequent recessions were relatively mild, lasting a year or so. Looking down the Gross National Product column, note that it dropped from 1937 to 1938, but recovered the very next year. It fell again after the Second World War in 1946 but recovered quickly the next year, being revived by increased personal consumption and gross private domestic investment. The overexpansion of capital goods slowed the economy in 1949 but only for one year.

Apart from the 1929-1933 period we have enjoyed a continuous period of expansion and prosperity.

Antirecession Measures

Prior to 1929 little was done to correct imbalances due to overproduction or underconsumption. The prevailing philosophy of laissez-faire was that time would correct imbalances. Overproduction of capital goods would result in falling prices, bankruptcies, and unemployment. At some point, lower production would adjust to consumption and a correction would take place. The economy would then move forward for approximately four years and plunge once more into its next business cycle.

The big depression following the stock market collapse of 1929 ended the laissez-faire theory. Self-correction did not take place. Unemployment increased. Bankruptcies followed one another. Securities tumbled almost to the vanishing point. Home and farm mortages were foreclosed. The currency system began to falter so that barter and local scrip replaced it in numerous areas. The political as well as the economic security of the nation began to deteriorate.

The New Deal and the modifications that followed abandoned laissez-faire. There emerged a philosophy that consumption must keep pace with production. Social Security and unemployment insurance followed. Credit purchases for consumers' goods burgeoned. In 1929 consumer credit amounted to approximately 7 billion dollars or $3\frac{1}{2}\%$ of the Gross National Product. By the end of 1967, it soared to 99 billion dollars. During this period the total credit structure rose sharply. By the end of 1967 the combined public and private debt amounted to *1 trillion, 430 billion dollars* vs 191 billion in 1929. The private portion alone stood at 1 trillion, 30 billion dollars, the balance being divided between the Federal government and state and local governments. We are living in a credit economy.

Who is responsible for the "new economics"? Some ascribe it

to President Franklin D. Roosevelt and the New Deal, etc.
Undoubtedly, it started with President Roosevelt. However, the
cause goes much deeper. The basis is grounded in the high-speed
efficiency of farm and factory. If the auto plants can assemble 8
million cars, and we can produce millions of radio and television
sets and millions of tons of food, etc., an economy must emerge
to consume these or else. In short, scientific development
created the "new" economics.

Today's economy is different from what it was 25 or 50
years ago. It is entirely different from what it was when our
forefathers came to this country to build a nation with their
own bare hands. Tomorrow's economy will be based on
conditions very different from those of today.

Depressions No More

If there is anything we cannot afford it is a depression. It is
too terrible to contemplate the wreckage it would create. Our
economy rests on a solid industrial foundation. Superimposed
on it is a delicate, intricate moneyed structure, created by
functionality. It is at the same time both its strength and a
source of danger. A telephone call and a signature on a piece of
paper makes it possible to transfer millions of dollars, even
billions, from one part of the world to another and smooth the
path for buyers and sellers.

During normal periods the piece of paper represents
ownership of great wealth, translated monetarily. However,
during a depression the same piece of paper can become
worthless.

What would happen to the 1 trillion 430 billion dollars'
worth of debt structure in a depression? What would happen to
the 700-odd billion dollars' worth of security values? These
assets, real and important normally, would shrink to fractions
of their value during a period of adversity. This is precisely what
happened during 1929-32. The pile is taller today and would
topple further. To get a rough idea of the consequences,

consider what did happen when a fuse blew in Canada that extinguished all the electric lights on the Eastern Seaboard of the United States in 1965.

Those who would like to simplify our economy by going back to the agricultural period when the ownership of land represented wealth are dreaming. It cannot be done. Along with and leading the rest of the world, our industrial structure has placed us in a new position. This is where we are, willy-nilly. We can only move forward—backward lies disaster.

Inflation

There is another aspect of the economy that materially affects investors. It is inflation. Just as growth and expansion are allies of the investor, inflation is his enemy. It robs him of his savings. It cheats him in his old age. It is a universal disease that has plagued organized society since its inception. It accompanies war, extending its devastation after the battle has ended.

Inflation is the result of buying power being created without a compensatory amount of consumers' goods. It can come about in many ways. It may follow a severe drought which reduces the amount of food and other necessities. It may take place in a nation where substantial savings are transferred abroad and hence are not invested in its own economy. As a result, the capital structure falls into such disrepair that it cannot produce sufficient goods. Inflation flourishes during wars when everyone is busily employed producing goods that do not enter the economy.

The Book of Genesis describes the results of the inflation that accompanied the seven lean years. The Egyptians had land, cattle, slaves and other forms of wealth. During the lean years their land produced no food. They were forced to go to the Pharaoh to buy his wheat, for he alone, thanks to Joseph, had bulging warehouses. Naturally, they had to pay dearly for the food. According to the Bible they gave him their money, cattle, slaves and finally their land.

A bizarre inflation struck Spain during the early part of the sixteenth century, at the pinnacle of its power. It had the largest hoard of gold and silver in the world, stolen from the Indians of Mexico and Peru. According to the Mercantile Theory then in vogue, that made it the richest nation. It paid little attention to producing goods. The sudden increase in the supply of the precious metals created a buying power that could not be satisfied by the meager supply of available goods, made scarce by continuous wars. As a result the country was wracked by a wave of inflation.

In our own country, inflation has visited us on numerous occasions. Following the Big Depression, there were a dozen years when there was a deflation of the currency. Starting in 1940, inflation emerged and soared during the war years. Thereafter it rose slowly but steadily, as can be seen from the table on page 168.

Referring to column 1, the cost of living stood at 59.7 during 1929 (1957-59 is 100). During the period that included the depression, 1930-39, it dropped 17%. Then followed the war years when it advanced 70%. Between 1950 and 1960 it rose another 21%. This rate was maintained until 1966. The rise during 1967 should be between 3 and 4%, based on the monthly reports. This is no doubt due to the pressure of the Vietnamese war. When it ends it is hoped that the increase will revert to a lower level.

The constant rise in the cost of living, even at the annual 2.1% rate, poses a serious problem for the investor. The cost of living has doubled since 1929. There is no reason to expect that the future will deal more kindly than the past. That is why this book opposes investing funds in fixed income situations, safe though they may be.

From time to time the Federal Reserve Bank has tried to stop or at least restrain the inflation by resorting to tight money and high interest rates. The last attempt was during 1966. Its only visible effect was to curtail building construction. Otherwise,

PRICES

Table B-45.–Consumer price indexes, by major groups, 1929-67

For city wage earners and clerical workers

(1957-59 = 100)

Year or month	All items	Food	Housing		Apparel and upkeep	Transportation	Medical care	Personal care	Reading and recreation	Other goods and services
			Total	Rent						
1929	59.7	55.6	—	85.4	55.3	—	—	—	—	—
1930	58.2	52.9	—	83.1	54.1	—	—	—	—	—
1931	53.0	43.6	—	78.7	49.2	—	—	—	—	—
1932	47.6	36.3	—	70.6	43.6	—	—	—	—	—
1933	45.1	35.3	—	60.8	42.1	—	—	—	—	—
1934	46.6	39.3	—	57.0	46.1	—	—	—	—	—
1935	47.8	42.1	56.3	56.9	46.5	49.4	49.4	42.6	50.2	52.7
1936	48.3	42.5	57.1	58.3	46.9	49.8	49.6	43.2	51.0	52.6
1937	50.0	44.2	59.1	60.9	49.3	50.6	50.0	45.7	52.5	54.0
1938	49.1	41.0	60.1	62.9	49.0	51.0	50.2	46.7	54.3	54.5
1939	48.4	39.9	59.7	63.0	48.3	49.8	50.2	46.5	54.4	55.4
1940	48.8	40.5	59.9	63.2	48.8	49.5	50.3	46.4	55.4	57.1
1941	51.3	44.2	61.4	64.3	51.1	51.2	50.6	47.6	57.3	58.2
1942	56.8	51.9	64.2	65.7	59.6	55.7	52.0	52.2	60.0	59.9

Year										
1943	60.3	57.9	64.9	65.7	62.2	55.5	54.5	57.6	65.0	63.0
1944	61.3	57.1	66.4	65.9	66.7	55.5	56.2	61.7	72.0	64.7
1945	62.7	58.4	67.5	66.1	70.1	55.4	57.5	63.6	75.0	67.3
1946	68.0	66.9	69.3	66.5	76.9	58.3	60.7	68.2	77.5	69.5
1947	77.8	81.3	74.5	68.7	89.2	64.3	65.7	76.2	82.5	75.4
1948	83.8	88.2	79.8	73.2	95.0	71.6	69.8	79.1	86.7	78.9
1949	83.0	84.7	81.0	76.4	91.3	77.0	72.0	78.9	89.9	81.2
1950	83.8	85.8	83.2	79.1	90.1	79.0	73.4	78.9	89.3	82.6
1951	90.5	95.4	88.2	82.3	98.2	84.0	76.9	86.3	92.0	86.1
1952	92.5	97.1	89.9	85.7	97.2	89.6	81.1	87.3	92.4	90.6
1953	93.2	95.6	92.3	90.3	96.5	92.1	83.9	88.1	93.3	92.8
1954	93.6	95.4	93.4	93.5	96.3	90.8	86.6	88.5	92.4	94.3
1955	93.3	94.0	94.1	94.8	95.9	89.7	88.6	90.0	92.1	94.3
1956	94.7	94.7	95.5	96.5	97.8	91.3	91.8	93.7	93.4	95.8
1957	98.0	97.8	98.5	98.3	99.5	96.5	95.5	97.1	96.9	98.5
1958	100.7	101.9	100.2	100.1	99.8	99.7	100.1	100.4	100.8	99.8
1959	101.5	100.3	101.3	101.6	100.6	103.8	104.4	102.4	102.4	101.8
1960	103.1	101.4	103.1	103.1	102.2	103.8	108.1	104.1	104.9	103.8
1961	104.2	102.6	103.9	104.4	103.0	105.0	111.3	104.6	107.2	104.6
1962	105.4	103.6	104.8	105.7	103.6	107.2	114.2	106.5	109.6	105.3
1963	106.7	105.1	106.0	106.8	104.8	107.8	117.0	107.9	111.5	107.1
1964	108.1	106.4	107.2	107.8	105.7	109.3	119.4	109.2	114.1	108.8
1965	109.9	108.8	108.5	108.9	106.8	111.1	122.3	109.9	115.2	111.4
1966	113.1	114.2	111.1	110.4	109.6	112.7	127.7	112.2	117.1	114.9
1967	116.3	115.2	114.3	112.4	114.0	115.9	136.7	115.5	120.1	118.2

(From *Economic Report of the President*, page 262)

businessmen were happy to borrow even at the high rates. They simply passed the increase on to the consumer. In effect, the tight money-high interest rate experiment added its own fuel to the inflation. It was allowed to die quietly. The cause of inflation is much too basic to be solved by such simple "aspirin remedies" as high interest or tight money.

The investor has greater need than ever before to protect his savings by a judicious investment policy. Equities, carefully purchased, have always been the best hedge. They still are.

Devaluation of Currency

In December 1967 the British pound was devalued by the government and the dollar was attacked. The British government was forced to devalue the pound after suffering many years of adverse export trade balances. As the result of the loss of colonies and greater trade freedom for the Empire, British imports exceeded exports. All the usual devices, such as borrowing abroad, selling foreign securities, and increasing interest rates were used. The final step had to be taken, which was the devaluation of the currency. Britain must import less, export more, and reduce its military expenditures.

The raid on the gold standard, which endangered the stability of the dollar, did not succeed. The future will depend on American fiscal policy. If the government continues the half measures that characterized the inaction of the past two decades, or if incorrect measures are taken, then devaluation will be inevitable.

Unlike Great Britain we have enjoyed a surplus of exports over imports. We have been selling more goods and services abroad than we have been importing. For the past two decades we have had a surplus each and every year, as large as $11.5 billion in 1947 and as little as $147 million in 1959. Despite this we have suffered an international dollar deficit for almost each and every year since 1950. To meet these deficits we have had to reduce our gold holdings from $21 billion in 1946 to $12.4 billion at the end of 1967. In addition, our indebtedness to foreign banks has increased to approximately $14 billion by the end of 1967.

The major drains on our export-import surplus have been: U.S. Government assistance, military expenditures abroad, and foreign investments abroad. These expenditures have exceeded our capability.

Can this situation be corrected by currency devaluation, going off the gold standard, or the use of some new kind of international currency? The nature of the cause supplies the answer. If we continue to suffer international deficits we will be in trouble. No nation, no matter how strong or important, can forever defy the logical laws of economics.

Do War Expenditures Help an Economy?

Many people believe that war aids an economy. They note that war preparation creates jobs and brings prosperity. This puts them in the dilemma of objecting to war yet quietly favoring it. Does the preparation for war or defense benefit an economy?

Historically, legislative bodies have always voted war funds lavishly even while their citizens languished in poverty. This resulted in "prosperity" before and during war periods.

The new "Keynsian" economics has changed all this. The Keynsian theory, simply stated, is that in an advanced industrial economy there is no need for depressions. When an economy lags the government simply takes up the slack by borrowing and spending. Our own economy has been operating on some such basis under both Democratic and Republican administrations though both parties publicly denounce Keynes.

Our economy has reached the advanced stage of development where it needs no artificial stimulation. What is required is careful planning to protect our raw materials, forests, water supply, and fresh air. The money spent for war could be expended to strengthen the nation by slum clearance and the elimination of poverty. All that wars do is accelerate inflation, destroy precious human beings, consume property and raw materials, and impoverish the nation.

Summary of Chapter

Prosperity should not be taken for granted. It has to be watched and nourished. In a wholesome economic climate, most industries do well. Production, consumption and re-investment of excess funds, or savings, are interrelated and inter-dependent. An expanding economy is the best protection for the investor. Government policy should be directed to correct imbalances as they develop. A sound investment policy is the individual's best protection against inflation.

10
Taxation

Every investor should know the rudiments of taxation as they apply to the ownership of securities. He need not try to become an expert. That is the job of his accountant. However, he should know the salient features which we present in this chapter.

Tax Exemption

Interest received from municipal and state bonds are exempt from Federal income taxation.

Interest received from Federal bonds are exempt from state and local taxes, but not from Federal income taxes.

Dividends received from certain (not all) public utilities and certain companies are partially tax exempt from income taxes. The amount varies with the utility. Consult your broker each year as to how much of the dividend from the utility is tax exempt.

Dividends

The first $100 of dividends received is exempt from Federal taxes. If the security is in the name of one spouse there is only one exemption. If the security is in both names or if both own securities then the first $200 is exempt.

All dividends above the $100 or $200 exemption are fully taxable and are treated as if they were salary or other income.

Capital Gains and Losses

Capital gains or losses are incurred only when a security is sold. If a security was held for 6 months or less before it was sold, the gain or loss is called *short-term*. If it was held for more than 6 months it is *long-term.*

Please note that the security has to be *sold* before a gain or loss can be established. The fact that a security rises or falls after being purchased does not establish a gain or loss for income tax purposes.

To simplify the discussion of how capital gains and losses are treated, they have been divided into two categories:

A. Tax Treatment of Capital Gains Only

If an individual has *only* capital gains and no losses, he is taxed as follows:

1. If they are short-term capital gains, he adds the amount to his other income and computes his taxes thereon. Technically, he lists the short-term capital gains in Schedule D and follows directions. In effect, short-term gains are fully taxable.

2. If the gain is long-term he makes two calculations. First, he adds half the gain to his other income and determines the tax on the total. He then makes a second calculation as follows: He determines the income tax on his other income (exclusive of capital gains). To that he adds 25% of his total long-term capital gain. He pays the smaller of the amounts in either the first or second calculations. The general idea is that the *maximum tax* on long-term capital gains is 25% of the long-term gain.

If a person has *both* long-term and short-term capital gains, he pays at the full rate on the short-term and on half of the long-term gain (or 25% of the long-term gain as previously explained.)

B. Tax Treatment of Capital Losses Only

If an individual has losses only, short-term or long-term he may reduce his regular income by the amount of the loss, but by not more than $1,000. If his loss in any one year exceeds

$1,000, he may reduce his other income by $1,000 and carry the excess forward to the following year. He may continue this until he has consumed all his losses.

Treatment of gains and losses

If a person has both gains and losses in the same year, long and short, he separates the longs from the shorts.

1. He subtracts the short-term gains from the short-term losses or vice versa, and gets one short-term figure. It may be a gain or loss.

2. He then subtracts the long-term gains from the long-term losses or vice versa, and gets one long-term figure. It may be a gain or loss.

If (1) and (2) are both gains, he follows A above.

If (1) and (2) are both losses, he follows B above.

If one is a gain and the other a loss, he subtracts the smaller from the larger figure and the result is a gain or loss, long or short, depending on the larger figure. If it is a gain he uses the method described in A. If a loss, method B.

Loss carry-forward

If a loss is carried forward it retains its original long or short position. Once a short-term, always a short-term. The same for long-term.

Stock Dividends, Splits, and Rights

There is no income tax on stock dividends or splits until the stock is sold. (There are exceptions in special cases.)

If rights are sold, they are treated as capital gains.

Deferring Income to Next Year

Capital gains and losses may be deferred to the following year by selling the stock *short* (against the box). If a stock is sold (short) in December and delivery is made in January of the following year, the gain or loss counts in the year that the delivery is made. This procedure cannot be used to "stretch" short-term into long-term. If the stock is short-term when sold short, it will be short-term capital gains when delivered. If long-term, when sold short it will be long-term when delivered.

Consult your broker, who is familiar with the practice.

Year-End Sales

To establish a loss, a security may be sold to the very last day of the year.

However, to establish a profit, a security must be sold so that the funds are available on or before the last day. This means that it must be sold at least 4 business days before the year end. Sales may be made on "next day" delivery basis. Your broker should be consulted for the last day that securities may be sold on the regular basis.

Contributions

If a contribution of stock is given to a tax-exempt charitable organization, the amount deductible for income tax purposes is the value of the stock at the time it is given, regardless of cost. Thus, if a security cost $1,000 and is given to a charitable institution when its market price is $5,000, the latter figure is deducted as a charitable contribution. No tax is paid on the $4,000 increase.

A good method is to sell the security in the name of the *charitable organization,* never in the taxpayer's name. The broker should be instructed to have the stock transferred to the charitable organization before making delivery. Brokers are quite familiar with the proper procedure.

Identification of Securities

A person who owns several lots of the same security, which he purchased at different dates and prices, may elect to sell any one of these, not necessarily the first purchased. This can be done by specifying the date of the purchase of the security *at the time the sale is made.* The date of purchase should appear *on the sales slip* and on the broker's monthly statement.

Gifts

Where a security is given as a gift, the donee (recipient) takes the cost and date of purchase of the donor, if he sells the security at a profit. However, if he sells it at less than the original cost, he takes the value of the security on the date the security is given as a gift or the original cost, whichever is lower.

Instead of giving cash as a gift, securities should be considered which have appreciated in value, provided the donee (recipient) is in a lower income tax bracket.

Inheritance

Where securities are inherited, the cost basis to the beneficiary is the value of the security on the date of death or one year thereafter, whichever had been selected by the executor when the estate was filed. The original cost is entirely irrelevant.

This places an obligation on the executor to be especially careful as to the date he selects. He should seek the advice of expert tax counsel.

Worthless Securities

If a security becomes worthless, a capital loss can be established in the year that it becomes worthless. If possible, it is best to sell the security, even for a few pennies, to avoid future problems with the Internal Revenue Bureau.

Summary of Chapter

An investor should not try to become a tax expert. However, he should be familiar with the overall treatment of capital gains and losses, gifts, charitable contributions, etc. This may save him many thousands of dollars in income taxes. For example, a person who gives generously to charity should be aware of the advantages of making contributions in securities that have appreciated in value, rather than in cash.

The investor should know enough to be able to discuss these matters with his attorney or accountant.

Glossary

Bear Market—A term used to describe a downward trend in security prices.

Blue Chip—Refers to a stock of a company of the highest quality, such as American Tel and Tel, Standard Oil of New Jersey, U.S. Steel, etc.

Bottom Out—After a security has reached its lowest price of the year, it may hover near this price for a period of time before it rises. It is establishing its bottom.

Bull Market—A term used to describe an upward trend in security prices.

Charting—Many security analysts make all kinds of graphs to guide them in their purchases and sales of securities. We have limited our charting to determine that price when a security which has been doing poorly will turn around and do well.

Diversification—Buying a great many securities in different industries so that the portfolio of investments represents a cross section of the entire economy.

Low of the Year—Refers to the lowest price at which a security sold that year. Most newspapers record this price daily. For previous years' highs and lows, consult Standard and Poor's sheets.

Portfolio—All the assets that a person owns. It includes cash in the bank, real estate, bonds, stocks, loans, coin collections, works of art (if purchased for investment).

Range—Refers to the highest and lowest price of a stock sold in any one year. For example, if the highest price at which a stock sold during 1967 was $75 and the lowest price $55, the range is 75-55. Range for stocks can be found in the Standard and Poor's reports of these stocks.

Selling Short—Securities may be bought first and sold later or sold first and bought later. There are restrictions on selling first, which are described on pages 132 and 133.

Spread—See Range.

Index

NOTES

NOTES

NOTES

NOTES

NOTES

NOTES

NOTES

NOTES